Witness and Service in North America

The
Mennonite Central Committee
Story Series

1. **From the Files of MCC** (1980)
   About the Origins, Russia (USSR), Refugee Work...
2. **Responding to Worldwide Needs** (1980)
   In Europe, the Middle East, Africa, Asia...
3. **Witness and Service in North America** (1980)
   Peace Witness, Mental Health, Voluntary Service...
4. **Something Meaningful for God** (1981)
   The Stories of Some Who Served with MCC...
5. **MCC Experiences: Issues and Choices** (1982)
   What Would You Do If...?

The Mennonite Central Committee Story
Volume 3. Documents

Witness and Service in North America

Cornelius J. Dyck, Editor
With Robert S. Kreider and John A. Lapp

HERALD PRESS
Scottdale, Pennsylvania
Kitchener, Ontario
1980

Library of Congress Cataloging in Publication Data

Main entry under title:
The Mennonite Central Committee story.
CONTENTS: v. 1. From the files of MCC.—v. 2. Responding to worldwide needs.—v. 3. Witness and service in North America.
1. Mennonite Central Committee—History—Sources. 2. Mennonites—Charities—History—Sources. I. Dyck, Cornelius J. II. Kreider, Robert S. III. Lapp, John Allen. IV. Mennonite Central Committee.
BX8128.W4M46 361.7'5 80-10975
ISBN 0-8361-1229-6 (v. 1)
ISBN 0-8361-1230-X (v. 2)
ISBN 0-8361-1231-8 (v. 3)

WITNESS AND SERVICE IN NORTH AMERICA

Published simultaneously in Canada by Herald Press, Kitchener, Ont. N2G 4M5
Library of Congress Catalog Card Number: 80-10975
International Standard Book Number: 0-8361-1231-8
Printed in the United States of America
Design by David Hiebert

15 14 13 12 11 10 9 8 7 6 5 4 3 2 1

Contents

Preface

When the idea of writing a history of the Mennonite Central Committee (MCC) was first raised with several of us who have been close to its life and work our response was not positive. Who would read a big volume about an agency that has become an institution and is simply taken for granted among Mennonites, and perhaps others? Besides, we do have A Ministry of Goodwill. A Short Account of Mennonite Relief, 1939-1949, written by Irvin B. Horst, (Akron, 1950), and the larger volume In The Name of Christ, by John D. Unruh (Scottdale, 1952), as well as other writings about the life and work of MCC. There seemed to be no shortage of available information.

In reflecting further on the question, however, it became clear to us that most of this literature was about MCC and that the readers had little opportunity to see for themselves how MCC worked, how its decisions were made, or how it all began. And so a proposal grew among us for the preparation of several smaller volumes which would tell the MCC story in a first-hand way and become a resource for other writers, for study groups in congregations and schools, as well as for private enjoyment.

For the present this has led to the preparation of five modest volumes, with the possibility of one or two more being added later. Of these five the first three form a unit which might simply be called "From the Files of the MCC", volume four contains the biographies of fifteen persons and, in some cases, spouses who have played a central role in MCC over many years, and volume five, which is still in preparation, might be called "What would you do if...?" because it presents specific situations from MCC experiences around the world in terms of crucial ethical and other issues and choices faced by MCC persons in their ministries.

The decisions about what and whom to include were difficult. In the first three volumes the rows of file boxes filled with interesting documents were almost overwhelming. Only a few could be selected, hopefully representative of the issues considered, and placed into context by brief introductory notations. Spelling and punctuation errors in the documents have been left as they were and have not been identified with the standard /sic/ to avoid excessive cluttering up of the manuscripts. Whom to include in a small collection of biographies proved equally difficult. It is hoped that it may become possible to compile another volume eventually of the great contributions made to MCC by non-North Americans. Only two of these biographies are included in volume four. The selection of issues and choices faced in sixty years of global activities was equally difficult, from the death of Clayton Kratz in Russia in 1920 to the involvement in Vietnam in the 1960s and 70s. To ask "What would you do..." in specific difficult situations can lead to spiritual growth and, perhaps, to words of counsel to MCC and persons serving with it.

The primary committee appointed by the MCC Executive Committee to guide this project consisted of Robert S. Kreider of Bethel College, North Newton, Kansas, John A. Lapp of Goshen College, Goshen, Indiana, and Cornelius J. Dyck of the Associated Mennonite Seminaries, Elkhart, Indiana who, in his capacity as Director of the Institute of Mennonite Studies was responsible for the implementation of the project. His debt to the wisdom and help of the other two members of the committee is here gratefully acknowledged. A larger committee was convened once for consultation, but written counsel was also received and appreciated. Its members were Paul Longacre and William T. Snyder of MCC, to whom special recognition is due for their strong support and encouragement, but also to Clarence Hiebert of Tabor College, Kenneth B. Hoover of Messiah College, J. M. Klassen and Dan Zehr of MCC (Canada), and Ted D. Regehr of Saskatoon, Saskatchewan.

Beyond these recognitions deep appreciation is expressed here to the many others who helped in one way or another, including Vernon Neufeld of Mennonite Mental Health Services for facilitating the selection of documents in that field, to Leonard Gross and Sharon Klingelsmith of the Archives of the Mennonite Church at Goshen, to typists and researchers Lois Janzen, Jennifer L. Dyck, Shirley B. Souder and particularly to Suzanne Keeney Lind and Sue Yoder for exceptional skills in research and in typing respectively. The writers of the biographies deserve their own special praise for erecting monuments in tribute to those whose lives they shared with us. The project could not have been undertaken without the financial and moral support of the MCC itself, through its Executive Committee and Annual Meeting, which is here gratefully acknowledged.

May all that has been done be "In The Name Of Christ", in His Spirit, and to His honor and glory.

Cornelius J. Dyck, Director
Institute of Mennonite Studies
June, 1979

1.
The Peace Witness of MCC

The Mennonite and Brethren in Christ commitment to Christian love and peacemaking is inherent in the very nature of MCC. The most recent MCC statement of faith calls Christian love the "central quality of the Christian faith /which/ becomes the basis of our relationship with all people.... Our response to human conflict, injustice, war and racial tension is based on the biblical teachings of nonviolence". (MCC Statement of Policy nd p. 2).

What has been implicit in the many service ministries has been explicit in the Peace Section established in 1942 to be concerned "with all matters relating to the historic Mennonite and Brethren in Christ nonresistant principles and their applications," a statement first used in the August 6, 1946 minutes of the Section. The Peace Section with its separate administration and sponsoring committee has served as the inter-Mennonite group working in such areas as witness to other Christians and governments, peace education and publication, relation to government especially the administration of alternative service, action projects ranging from official statements to peace teaching teams and reconciliation ministries in conflict situations.

The following documents illustrate some of the Peace Section activities and indicate the development of policy and program. Readers interested in fuller explanation should see works cited in the bibliographical references.

Structure and Commitments: The structure and mission of the Peace Section has been outlined in guiding principles first stated in 1942 with revisions in 1946, 1959, 1961, 1969, 1971, and 1974. There have been few substantive changes through the years although the structure has been enlarged and formalized. Reading 1 was adopted by the section in 1968 and the MCC at its annual meeting January, 1969.

Reading 1

"Guiding Principles for the MCC Peace Section," MCC Annual Meeting, January 24-25, 1969.

A. Delegation of Responsibility

1. In spirit and purpose, the MCC Peace Section is an agency at the service of MCC constituent and related groups through their peace, mission, and service agencies. Administratively and legally, the Peace Section derives its mandate

from the Mennonite Central Committee.

2. The Peace Section receives recommendations, advice, and counsel directly from constituent and related groups through their peace committees, Council of Mission Board Secretaries, or other channels.

3. The Peace Section is responsible to report its program operations and program projections to the MCC Annual Meeting for review and approval. Within the program policies and budget approved by the MCC Annual Meeting, the Peace Section is responsible for operating its program.

B. Scope and Areas of Interest

The Section's particular areas of interest shall be all matters relating to the historic Mennonite and Brethren in Christ nonresistant principles and their applications. Specifically, this shall include: (1) war and revolution, (2) industrial relations, (3) church and state relations, (4) race relations, (5) international affairs, (6) capital punishment and penal reform, (7) problems of urbanization, (8) poverty and affluence, (9) other areas of peace or related concerns may be subsequently added to the responsibility of this section upon the recommendation of the Section, in consultation with the constituent agencies and approval of the MCC.

C. Functions

1. Formulation of basic attitudes and philosophy, and expression of these in statements of position.

2. Study and research in the assigned areas, including assembling of information on current trends and developments.

3. Preparation and publication of literature and other materials in the fields of interest: pamphlets, books, articles, audio-visuals, etc.

4. Provide information to the constituent groups on current events and developments, bibliography, etc.

5. Clearing center service for the interests and activities of the constituent groups in the areas of peace and social concerns.

6. Furnish counsel and professional resources to other departments of MCC and other church agencies in equipping personnel for peace witness and in dealing with questions arising out of programs.

7. Representation in meetings and organizations relating to Peace Section concerns.

8. Provide representation to the Federal governments for any or all constituent groups as may be desired and authorized. However, this service shall not be understood to prevent any single group from presenting its concerns or convictions to the government directly.

9. Oversight of cooperative Selective Service processing

and decisions on project approval; provide resources for Selective Service counseling.

10. In consultation with Council of Mission Board Secretaries, be especially alert to ways of coordinating with, supporting and serving Mennonite and Brethren in Christ churches and missions overseas in cultivating their witness to peace and social concerns (e.g., by correspondence, literature, special commissioners, and other means).

11. In consultation with other church agencies active in the ministry to students, be alert to ways of coordinating, supporting, and serving in the areas of Peace Section concerns.

12. Cultivating the Christian peace witness among other Christians at home and abroad.

D. Relations to Peace Section Constituent Groups

1. The work of the Peace Section is to serve the constituent groups by supplementing their own work in this area or by working in concert with them. It is not to displace nor hamper their work. Each group is free to undertake any activity which it may desire, and give whatever individual witness it feels called to give subject only to courtesy, and cooperation in matters which affect other groups and their interests.

2. The Peace Section shall be alert to developments in its field of concern and service and take the initiative in suggesting to its constituency matters of importance for consideration and action.

3. The fruits of the work of the Section shall be made available to the constituent groups for whatever use they may see fit. The archives and files shall be accessible to properly accredited representatives at all times.

4. The Section will speak for the constituent groups in a representative capacity only when and so far as it is requested and authorized to do so by the groups.

5. The Section will serve any constituent groups on request in any field of interest within the limits of policy and capacity.

E. Doctrinal Position* /*This section is quoted verbatim from the present "Guiding Principles for the MCC Peace Section," revised January 19, 1961./

The doctrinal position underlying the work of the Peace Section includes the following statements from the Declaration of Christian Faith and Commitment, adopted by a study conference of representatives of substantially all North American Brethren in Christ and Mennonite groups held at Winona Lake, Indiana, November 9-12, 1950. The entire Winona Lake Declaration is hereby accepted as a policy for Peace Section work.

"1. It is our faith that one is our Master, even Christ,

to whom alone supreme loyalty and obedience is due, who is our only Saviour and Lord.

"2. It is our faith that by the renewing grace of God which makes us new creatures in Christ, and alone thereby, we can through the power of the indwelling Spirit live the life of holy obedience and discipleship to which all the sons of God are called, for His grace does forgive and heal the penitent sinner and brings us to a new life of fellowship with Him and with one another.

"3. It is our faith that redeeming love is at the heart of the Gospel, coming from God and into us to constrain us to love Him and our neighbor, and that such love must henceforth be at the center of every thought and act.

"4. It is our faith that Christ has established in His church a universal community and brotherhood within which the fullness of Christ's reign must be practiced, into which the redeemed must be brought, and from which must go out into all human society the saving and healing ministry of the Gospel.

"5. It is our faith that the life of love and peace is God's plan for the individual and the race, and that therefore discipleship means the abandonment of hatred, strife, and violence in all human relations, both individual and social."

Further, the Peace Section stands on the platform that all our peace principles are rooted in Christ and His Word, that our peace testimony must be a part of our testimony to the Gospel, and that it is clearly distinguished from humanitarian or moralistic pacifism. It considers it to be the obligation of the church to propagate the testimony of love, peace, and nonresistance as a part of its total ministry and mission, so that the work of the Peace Section at home or abroad is seen as a part of the work of the church, and is not to be divorced from it. When the peace witness is given to non-Christians, it shall be done as part of the total Christian faith and way of life and thus commend the Gospel to those who have not yet come to Christ in faith.

F. Membership and Meetings

1. Members shall be chosen on the basis of their interest, willingness, and ability to serve actively in the work of the Section. The Section will meet as a committee of the whole at least three times annually, with expenses for attendance to be paid by the appropriate sponsoring agencies or groups.

2. Members of the Peace Section shall be chosen as follows: (a) Two members elected by MCC. (b) One or two members elected by council of Mission Board Secretaries. (c) One member each may be named by the peace committee or comparable agency of the constituent or related groups, which

regularly contribute financially and participate actively in it. (d) The Peace Section may elect up to three members-at-large.

3. All interested groups shall be invited to appoint representatives to a General Assembly which shall meet at least annually to review Peace Section and related concerns. These members shall receive periodic Peace Section mailings and have access to other Peace Section services. Expenses for attendance at meetings of the General Assembly shall be paid by the appropriate sponsoring agencies and groups.

4. The MCC Executive Secretary shall provide liaison between the Peace Section and other departments of MCC, and be available to staff for counsel and guidance.

5. Membership on the Peace Section shall be for a term of three years except for members named by constituent groups which may follow another pattern.

G. Officers

1. The following officers shall be elected annually by the Section. Chairman, Vice-chairman, and Recording Secretary.

2. The Executive Officer of the Peace Section shall be appointed by the MCC upon recommendation of the Section.

3. The Peace Section may secure and appoint other staff members. These shall be processed through MCC Personnel Services.

H. Finances

1. An annual budget shall be prepared by the Peace Section in consultation with the MCC Executive Committee and submitted with the total MCC budget to the MCC Annual Meeting for approval.

2. MCC shall be primarily responsible to raise the funds needed for the approved budget.

3. The finances shall be handled by the MCC Treasurer's Office.

I. Any changes in these Guiding Principles shall be approved by the MCC Annual Meeting, with proposals circulated in advance to MCC members, upon recommendation from Peace Section, in consultation with MCC Executive Committee.

* * *

Mennonites have frequently found themselves struggling for an identity between groups which emphasize doctrinal correctness and those whose concern is more ethical and historical. The peace section organized a Study Conference on Nonresistance held at Winona Lake, Indiana, November 9-12, 1950. Reading 2, signed by 62 delegates from Mennonite and

and Brethren in Christ Churches of North America, has served as a theological basis for peace section work.

Reading 2

A declaration of Christian faith and commitment... Winona Lake, Indiana, November 9-12, 1950.

I

At this mid-point of the 20th century, at a critical time in a generation marked by wide-spread and disastrous wars and shadowed by the threat of still more ruinous warfare, this conference of delegated representatives from the Mennonite and Brethren in Christ churches of the United States and Canada unites in a renewed declaration of faith in Jesus Christ, the Prince of Peace, in His Gospel, and in His power to redeem and transform in life and in human society all those who receive Him as Saviour and Lord and are thus born anew by the Spirit of God. It also unites in a deeper commitment to follow Christ in full discipleship in the way of peace and love, the way of nonresistance and peacemaking. In this conference we have seen anew the high calling of the sons of God, having been confronted with the absolute claims which Christ makes upon us. We acknowledge these claims in full, and have sought to trace the meaning of His Lordship and the consequences of our commitment in earnest and informed conversation together and in urgent prayer to God for grace and light, seeking to know His will for us in this day.

In our common consideration we have come to certain united convictions expressed in the following declarations which we now humbly send as our message to all our churches both in America and throughout the world as well as to all others who own Christ as Lord. To our brethren we say, this is the day for us to take a clear and unwavering stand on the great essentials of the Gospel and Christian discipleship. It is a day in which to demonstrate and proclaim courageously and unflinchingly this redemptive Gospel and this life of love and service in its fullness and its glory. Let us do so in united purpose with one heart and voice, trusting in the power of God and the companionship of our Lord who has promised to be with us alway.

II

1. It is our faith that one is our Master, even Christ, to whom alone supreme loyalty and obedience is due, who is our only Saviour and Lord.

2. It is our faith that by the renewing grace of God which makes us new creatures in Christ, and alone thereby,

we can through the power of the indwelling Spirit live the life of holy obedience and discipleship to which all the sons of God are called, for His grace does forgive and heal the penitent sinner and brings us to a new life of fellowship with Him and with one another.

3. It is our faith that redeeming love is at the heart of the Gospel, coming from God and into us to constrain us to love Him and our neighbor, and that such love must henceforth be at the center of every thought and act.

4. It is our faith that Christ has established in His church a universal community and brotherhood within which the fullness of Christ's reign must be practiced, into which must go out into all human society the saving and healing ministry of the Gospel.

5. It is our faith that the life of love and peace is God's plan for the individual and the race, and that therefore discipleship means the abandonment of hatred, strife and violence in all human relations, both individual and social.

III

These declarations of faith give no blueprint for peace nor do they assume that human endeavor alone can bring about a warless world within history, for only when men come under the Lordship of Christ can they make peace and fulfill the prayer of our Lord, "Thy Kingdom come, Thy will be done on earth as in heaven." They do, however, require certain attitudes, duties and ministries of us, to which we do here by God's grace declare our adherence and our determination to undertake in His name.

1. Our love and ministry must go out to all men regardless of race or condition, within or without the brotherhood, whether friend or foe, and must seek to bring the Gospel and all its benefits to every one. Race or class prejudice must never be found among us.

2. We do recognize fully that God has set the state in its place of power and ministry. But, recognizing the relative and conditional validity of any particular form of government and of concrete legislative, executive and judicial acts, we hold that we must judge all things in the light of God's Word and see that our responses to the relativities of the state and its workings are always conformed to the absolutes of Christian discipleship and love. We acknowledge our obligation to witness to the powers that be of the righteousness which God requires of all men, even in government, and beyond this to continue in earnest intercession to God on their behalf.

3. We do have the responsibility to bring to the total social order of which we are a part, and from which we re-

ceive so much, the utmost of which we are capable in Christian love and service. Seeking for all men first the kingdom of God and His righteousness, we must hold together in one united ministry the evangelism which brings men to Christ and the creative application of the Gospel to cultural, social and material need; for we find that the true and ultimate goal of evangelism is the Christianization of the whole of life and the creation of the fully Christian community within the fellowship of faith. For this reason the social order, including our own segment of it, must be constantly brought under the judgment of Christ.

4. We cannot be satisfied to retain for ourselves and our communities alone, in any kind of self-centered and isolated enjoyment, the great spiritual and material goods which God has bestowed upon us, but are bound in loving outreach to all to bear witness and to serve, summoning men everywhere to the life of full discipleship and to the pursuit of peace and love without limit. Separately and together we must use every feasible way and facility for this ministry: the spoken and written word; the demonstration of holiness and love in family, church, and community; relief work and social service; and all other ways. We must enlist many more of our people in such witness and service, both as a major purpose of their life and for specific projects and terms. Especially now must Christian love and redemptive action find expression in our ministry of service, when men are turning more and more to the use of force and war in futile attempts to solve the urgent problems of our world. In this service our youth can play a great part. They should give themselves to it in large numbers, both for shorter terms and in lifetime dedication.

5. Parallel with this we must practice an increasingly sharper Christian control of our economic, social and cultural practices among ourselves and toward others, to make certain that love truly operates to work no ill to our neighbor, either short-range or long-range. Knowing how much the selfishness, pride and greed of individuals, groups, and nations, which economic systems often encourage, help to cause carnal strife and warfare, we must see to it that we do not contribute thereto, whether for the goals of direct military operations or to anything which destroys property or causes hurt or loss of human life.

6. While rejecting any social system or ideology such as atheistic communism, which opposes the Gospel and would destroy the true Christian faith and way of life, we cannot take any attitude or commit any act contrary to Christian love against those who hold or promote such views or practices, but must seek to overcome their evil and win them through the Gospel.

7. We cannot compromise with war in any form. In case of renewed compulsion by the state in any form of conscription of service or labor, money or goods, including industrial plants, we must find ways to serve our countries and the needs of men elsewhere, in ways which will give significant and necessary benefits, which will keep our Christian testimony uncompromised, particularly with respect to war and which will make possible a faithful representation of Christ and His love. We cannot therefore participate in military service in any form. We cannot have any part in financing war operations or preparations through war bonds. We cannot knowingly participate in the manufacture of munitions, weapons, and instruments of war or destruction. We cannot take part in scientific, educational, or cultural programs designed to contribute to war, or in any propaganda or activity that tends to promote ill-will or hatred among men or nations. We must rather foster good will, understanding, and mutual regard and help among all nations, races, and classes. And we cannot as churches lend ourselves to the direct administration of conscription or state compulsion, seeking rather to find voluntary patterns of service through which the demands of the state may be both satisfied and transcended, and going with our men in whatever civilian service they give.

8. If war does come with its possible serious devastation from bombings or other forms of destruction, such as atomic blasts, germ warfare, poison gas, etc., we will willingly render every help which conscience permits, sacrifically and without thought of personal safety, so long as we thereby help to preserve and restore life and not to destroy it.

IV

While we are deeply grateful to God for the precious heritage of faith including the principle of love and nonresistance,* which our Swiss, Dutch, and German Anabaptist-Mennonite forefathers purchased for us by their faith, obedience, and sacrifice, and which we believe is again expressed in the above declarations and commitments, we are convinced that this faith must be repossessed personally by each one out of his own reading and obeying of God's Word, and must ever be spelled out in life practice anew. Hence, we summon our brotherhood to a deeper mastery of the Scriptures as the infallible revelation of God's will for us, and to a finding afresh under Holy Spirit guidance of its total message regarding Christ's way and its application in our present world.

We humbly confess our inadequacies and failures both in understanding and in following this way, knowing well that we have come short both in demonstration and proclamation of Christian love. As we renew our commitment of discipleship and ambassadorship for Christ, we know how much we need God's grace and each other's help in the fellowship of His body in learning and obeying. Let us therefore stand together and go on together in His name and for His cause.

*A faith universally held by the Mennonites of all lands for the first three centuries of our history and continuously confessed by all groups in North America until this day.

Conference Delegates:

Harold S. Bender, Goshen, IN; Ford Berg, Birdsboro, PA; Eli J. Bontreger, Shipshewana, IN; B. J. Braun, Dinuba, CA; Aldine Brenneman, Harrisonburg, VA; H. A. Brunk, Harrisonburg, VA; George L. Classen, Yale, SD; Harry A. Diener, Hutchinson, KS; Elmer Ediger, Newton, KS; Paul E. Engle, Upland, CA; Henry A. Fast, North Newton, KS; J. Herbert Fretz, Freeman, SD; J. Winfield Fretz, North Newton, KS; Albert Gaeddert, Inman, KS; Melvin Gingerich, Goshen, IN; Erwin C. Goering, North Newton, KS; Noah Good, Lancaster, PA; Paul T. Guengerich, Parnell, IA; John A. Harder, Yarrow, B.C.; Orlando Harms, Hillsboro, KS; R. L. Hartzler, Bloomington, IL; Robert W. Hartzler, Goshen, IN; Guy F. Hershberger, Goshen, IN; John H. Hess, Kitchener, Ont.; Anson G. Horner, Kokomo, IN; John L. Horst, Scottdale, PA; John A. Hostetler, Scottdale, PA; C. N. Hostetter, Jr., Grantham, PA; B. B. Janz, Coaldale, Alberta; Robert Kreider, Bluffton, OH; John E. Lapp, Lansdale, PA; Ernest W. Lehman, Akron, PA; Jesse B. Martin, Waterloo, Ontario; Orie O. Miller, Akron, PA; Rollin W. Moser, Nappanee, IN; William Neufeld, San Jose, CA; Arnold Nickel, Henderson, NE; Paul A. Nigh, Hagersville, Ontario; S. F. Pannabecker, Chicago, IL; Shem Peachey, Springs, PA; P. K. Regier, Newton, KS; David P. Reimer, Giroux, Manitoba; C. J. Rempel, Kitchener, Ontario; George J. Rempel, Meade, KS; John G. Rempel, Rosthern, Sask.; J. A. Ringenberg, Ft. Wayne, IN; David Schulz, Altona, Man.; Maynard Shelly, Newton, KS; J. Harold Sherk, Akron, PA; Richard Showalter, Reedley, CA; Donovan E. Smucker, Chicago, IL; J. N. Smucker, Chicago, IL; V. K. Snyder, Kitchener, Ont.; E. G. Steiner, Berne, IN; Milo D. Stutzman, Kingman, Alta.; E. J. Swalm, Duntroon, Ont.; Elmer G. Swartzendruber, Wellman, IA; John B. Toews, Hillsboro, KS; Dwight M. Wiebe, Hillsboro, KS; Allan A. Wiggers, Halstead, KS; Arverd Wiggers, Galva, KS.

* * *

Statements and Petitions to the American Government: MCC has intersected with government from its earliest activities both at home and abroad. Beginning in the late 1930's, MCC as the Mennonite link to the other Historic Peace Churches (Church of the Brethren and Society of Friends) actively participated in the development of alternative service with government agencies. At each step of the way, the relationship included a testimony against war and conscription as national policy with an attempt to find some way of civilian rather than military service.

Reading 3 is a letter from the three peace churches to President Roosevelt in 1940 appealing for alternative service should conscription be imposed. Reading 4 and 5 are statements to congressional committees in 1947 and 1948 opposing conscription and war. There have been numerous similar statements but this illustrates the type of statement given each year the military draft was considered up to as recent as 1971. Reading 6 shows how the involvement of MCC in service activities and the military action of the American government conflicted and led to several vigorous statements opposing war, in this case in Vietnam.

Reading 3

The Honorable Franklin D. Roosevelt January 10, 1940
The President of the United States
The White House
Washington, D.C.

Dear Mr. President:

On February 12, 1937, you graciously received representatives of the Society of Friends, the Mennonite Church, and the Church of the Brethren, who presented to you statements expressing the historic and unbroken convictions of these groups against war, and their devotion to peace and goodwill. These attitudes grew out of deep religious convictions, based on the spirit and teachings of Jesus, and are a part of a way of life which we believe cherishes the highest values for all men. Today we again submit to you our concerns in view of present world conditions.

We desire, first of all, to express our deep appreciation for your repeated effort to prevent the European war, our warm support of your confident insistence that the United States shall not be drawn into this conflict, and our hope that opportunity will arise for our nation to cooperate with other neutral nations in offering mediation or other peace-promoting techniques toward the earliest possible establishment of peace. We have also warmly appreciated your personal interest in the large number of political and racial refugees whose relief and resettlement are so urgent a present obligation for all men of goodwill. Your recent challenging appeal for humanitarian relief to European war sufferers has likewise won the hearty response of our groups. Our own organizations are definitely planning to contribute to such projects in the future, as in the past, not only with the desire to minister to human need, but also to keep vivid the vision of a better way of life than that of intolerance, persecution and war.

Opportunities and responsibilities of relief and rehabilitation for the war sufferers in Spain and elsewhere have come to us recently through the American Friends Service Committee and the service agencies of the Mennonite Church and Church of the Brethren. Our Spanish relief program, after more than two years, is probably drawing to a close, but relief responsibilities in China continue. Refugee colonies in Paraguay and Brazil still require our care and support. Just now we are being asked by interested American groups to assume important new responsibilities for the many tragic Polish war sufferers, and our representatives are now in Europe to investigate, and if possible, to inaugurate this project.

If, in spite of all efforts to maintain neutrality, the tragic day should come when our beloved nation is drawn into war, we should expect to continue our work for suffering humanity, and to increase its scope because of the greater need at home and abroad. Such service would permit those whose conscientious convictions forbid participation in war in any form to render constructive service to their country and to the world. We appear today chiefly to discuss with you plans to provide for this alternative service as it may relate to possible conscription, reserving the privilege to offer at a later date a supplementary memorandum dealing with other types of conscientious objectors.

As you know, in the last war the United States Government finally authorized such non-military humanitarian service to be substituted for military service, and furloughed conscientious objectors to this relief work or to farm labor. But this arrangement was provided only after months of confusion and distress, and only after repeated conferences between our representatives and officials of the War Department, because of the lack of any previously established policy. Since we understand that plans are now being formulated for mobilization of the nation's man power if war should come and since the need for dealing with conscientious objectors would again emerge to confront Government agencies, we venture to suggest the advantage of advance discussion of the problem with the appropriate officials. We should much appreciate the opportunity for such discussion and are prepared to make concrete proposals to such officials regarding procedures for handling conscientious objectors and types of service which might be provided. In this connection we also venture to suggest the desirability of again setting up a civilian agency for dealing with this problem. There is a precedent for this in the action of President Wilson in 1918.

We have come to you, Mr. President, with these requests, because our previous conversations with you have persuaded us that you both understand and appreciate the position of the historic peace churches. Our desire is to cooperate in finding the best solution to the problem of the conscientious objector, and it is even more to render as loyal citizens the highest type of constructive service we can to our country and to the world.

Faithfully yours,
FOR THE SOCIETY OF FRIENDS
Rufus Jones
Walter C. Woodward
FOR THE MENNONITE CHURCH
P. C. Hiebert
Harold S. Bender
E. L. Harshbarger
FOR THE CHURCH OF THE BRETHREN
Rufus D. Bowman
Paul H. Bowman

Reading 4

STATEMENT ON CONSCRIPTION FOR MILITARY TRAINING AND PROVISIONS FOR CONSCIENTIOUS OBJECTORS

Submitted to the President's Advisory Commission on Universal Training

April 10, 1947

We appreciate greatly this privilege of appearing before you on behalf of the Mennonite Central Committee and the Mennonite and affiliated bodies which it represents, to register with you our deep conviction that the Congress should not adopt any program of compulsory military training, and to speak on behalf of provisions for the Christian conscientious objector in connection with the possible passage of such legislation.

*******In as much as our churches have furnished about forty per cent of all conscientious objectors inducted into Civilian Public Service under the provisions of the Burke-Wadsworth bill during the recent war, and inasmuch as our service organization, the Mennonite Central Committee, was responsible, under Selective Service authorization, for the administration of C. P. S. camps and units taking care of over 5,800 inductees, we desire to offer some suggestions for the consideration of the Commission.

Before we do so, may we express our appreciation for the provisions of the Burke-Wadsworth bill and for the executive directives from the office of the President which made possible the Civilian Public Service program which was put into operation in 1940 and continued until March 31, 1947. The first director of Selective Service, Dr. Clarence Dykstra, and his successor, Maj. General Lewis B. Hershey, and their staffs, did well, we believe, under the limitations imposed upon them by the law and by war-time conditions, and our relations with them were most cordial. They enabled us to meet the basic requirements of conscience on our part as well as to permit our drafted men to perform a significant service to the nation.

May we also express the hope that *********certain improvements may be made over the former legislative and executive provisions for conscientious objectors, some of which were suggested in Attorney General Biddle's annual report.

We suggest for your serious consideration the following points:

(1) That complete exemption from the draft be provided for all those whose conscience sincerely forbids them to accept any form of conscription, and for whom the only alternative is prison. America, the historic land of freedom of conscience, should not demean herself by forcing such a minority into federal penitentiaries. Great Britain in this respect was ahead of the United States in the recent war, having made provision for complete exemption upon the basis of the judgment of a tribunal.

(2) That full provision be made for completely non-military training or service under civilian direction for those whose conscience forbids them to have any part in war or preparation for it, or any type of training related to the military security of the nation.

(3) That the entire process of selection, induction, and administration of conscientious objectors in training or service be completely divorced from the military program and any training for military security. It is no reflection on the high character of the individuals involved to say that in our judgment it is basically inconsistent and undesirable to assign to men charged with raising or training military forces, or providing for training men for national security, the administration of conscientious objectors to military service or to such training. We urge that any new universal training bill or executive order should provide that agencies or individuals attached to the armed forces or involved in the universal military training program in any way should not participate in the C. O. program in any form.

(4) While we agree that the federal government should assume basic administrative responsibility for an alternative service and training program for conscientious objectors, we urge that adequate provision be made for training or service projects wholly as under the administration of church agencies

and for the release of inductees to these projects at their request. We can speak only for ourselves in this, although no doubt other church agencies will have similar desires. We hope that the record of the Mennonite Central Committee, and of the Mennonite inductees in the recent Civilian Public Service Program covering a period of almost six years, may warrant the Government in placing continued trust in us for the operation of service projects in peace time. We believe that a wholly government-administered program in which the church would have only a chaplaincy relationship similar to that now prevailing in the army, with segregation by denominations, would be unnecessary as well as unsatisfactory, both to the Government and to us. We feel deeply on this as a matter of religious and conscientious concern, and appeal to the Commission to recommend a plan which would not force us and other conscientious persons into the painful position of choosing between our loyalty to our Government and emigration or prison. We believe further that our position on this point merits consideration inasmuch as it is clear that the great majority of eighteen-year-old conscientious objectors inducted (actually over eighty per cent) were members of Mennonite groups and that this proportion would probably continue in case of peacetime conscription for universal training. For your service in consideration of this matter we attach to our testimony a Statement of Policy of the Mennonite Central Committee used in the operation of Civilian Public Service work, issued in 1943.

(5) That the war time policy of no maintenance or wage grants for C.P.S. men be discontinued, and that in the future those agencies, either public or private, which profit from the labor of inductees, provide both maintenance and wage allowances on a basis to be determined or approved by the Government,**********

These constitute our suggestions which we hope will receive favorable consideration in the final decisions of your Commission. We are prepared to confer further with any members of the Commission regarding them or any point in the entire C. O. issue.

Respectfully submitted on behalf of the Mennonite Central Committee, with the constituent Mennonite and Brethren in Christ bodies which it represents.

H. S. Bender, Goshen, Indiana
The Mennonite Church
Assistant Secretary, Mennonite Central Committee
Chairman of the Peace Section of the Mennonite Central Committee

Albert M. Gaeddert, Inman, Kansas
The General Conference of the Mennonites of North America

Vice-Chairman of the Peace Section of the Mennonite Central Committee

Reading 5

A STATEMENT OF POSITION TO THE ARMED SERVICES COMMITTEE OF THE UNITED STATES SENATE CONCERNING PEACETIME CONSCRIPTION AND THE CHRISTIAN CONSCIENCE AGAINST WAR

Presented to this committee at the public hearing March 31, 1948, Washington, D.C., on behalf of the Mennonite Central Committee, Akron, Pennsylvania

I am Rev. Don. E. Smucker of Chicago, Ill., a teacher in the Mennonite Biblical Seminary. I am the duly authorized representative of the Mennonite Central Committee whose supporting churches number over 125,000 baptized members in the U. S.

It is with a heavy heart that our organization makes this witness to the elected representatives of the United States. This is true because we share the concern of our fellow-citizens over the dangers of this disturbed era; this time of wars and rumors of wars. We have been here before in other moments testifying to the nature of the Gospel as we understand it. And, also testifying to our experience in many different situations. Today's testimony is part of an unbroken witness since coming to America in 1685; a witness extending back to the days of the Reformation in Holland and Switzerland when the church was started.

Few Christians have known the sting of war and the crushing effects of conscription better than the various groups of Mennonites. Since Reformation days we have been refugees from bitter persecution of ruthless governments and intolerant religious movements.

In more recent times the most perfect illustration of our witness has been the situation in Russia. The Mennonites of South Russia were of original Dutch stock, coming to Russia by way of Prussia where they had not liked German militarism. When the Czars withdrew military exemption in 1874, 10,000 came to Kansas, Nebraska, the Dakotas and Minnesota. Under the Communist regimes thousands perished. Later, in the years 1923-30, 25,000 of our people left the Soviet Union, going to Canada, Mexico and Paraguay. Finally, in one of the thrilling yet sorrowful stories of the second World War, 30,000 Mennonites were able to leave Russia in 1943. Of these 20,000 have disappeared. 10,000 are accounted for in refugee camps in Denmark and in new migrations to Paraguay. A very small number have come here to the USA. Indeed, the Mennonites knew the meaning of brutality, war, conscription and dictatorship throughout Europe but particularly under the Czars and Communists of Russia.

II

For the above reasons we are in no mood to deny the seriousness of the crisis; not to underestimate the precious reality of freedom of conscience. On the other hand, throughout our history we have not permitted political and military circumstances to alter the unchanging commandments of Jesus Christ as we have read them in the New Testament. As a matter of fact, Christ, Himself, did not base His work for us on our reaction to Him. The Apostle Paul observed this fact when he wrote: "But God commended His love toward us in that while we were yet sinners, Christ died for us." The Apostle John declares that "God so loved the world that He gave His only begotten Son that whosoever believeth in Him should not perish but have everlasting life." Thus, God's motive in sending Christ was love.

And it is precisely this principle which is basic in the Christian life. We, too, are called to forgive our enemies, to go the second mile, be long-suffering, love our neighbors as ourselves, forgive seventy times seven, overcome evil with good, to embark on a ministry of reconciliation through Christ beyond racial, class and national barriers and to obey God rather than man.

III

All this is not in conflict with good citizenship but is necessary for it. Our own experience as a Christian community has shown that disaster results whenever nations ignore these basic Christian teachings. All over the world nations have perished by disobeying God and flaunting the Christian law of love. Today the teachings of Jesus Christ and over 400 years experience with war and conscription recall us to the urgency of these lessons of faith and painful experience.

Conscription for war we consider unChristian. And what is wrong is dangerous and suicidal.

Various nations have always thought they could be exempt from God's judgment. They believed they could avoid reaping chaos from the seed of militarism. Whatever the short-term situation, the long-term answer is clear: "they that take the sword perish by the sword." Therefore, this great nation dare not seek exception from this terrible moral fact. The Gospel suggests no exceptions. History offers no exceptions. America has had a special cup of blessings because it sought its destiny apart from brutality, conscription, dictatorship and the suppression of liberties.

We are deeply sympathetic with the profound dilemmas and agonizing challenges which men of state are facing. Surely now is not the time for glibness since the peril is real and the problem baffling. As we face these issues today people are fearful; people are developing deep despair and bitterness as they think of a third world war in such a short time after the second costly global bleeding.

Yet the Mennonite churches believe that God is using this crisis to force a decision. Jesus said: "Ye cannot serve God and mammon." (Matt. 6:24) This choice is the supreme issue of our time. No answer including Christ's answer is easy or safe. But the safest place in the world is the doing of God's will as revealed in the Lord Jesus Christ.

Therefore we respectfully declare that further extension of the power of the state over the lives of men through military training is not desirable; that government control of immature young people is undesirable; that God does have a way of dealing with evil doers through forgiving love and moral judgment; that history is a clear warning against this policy. This hearing is taking place three days after Easter . . . . . This reveals that Christ is more powerful than death itself. Mr. Chairman, we, therefore, are opposed to both selective service and universal military training as unChristian and dangerous in the light of history. Constantly in our prayers and now with our direct testimony, we ask you not to employ evil as an answer to evil.

During the second World War we appreciated the goodwill of government officials toward our leaders and our young people facing the draft. The attached statement contains the relevent parts of our testimony to the President's Advisory Commission on Universal Training, April 10, 1947. It will clarify our reaction to this experience under conscription. Finally, we are attaching a statement made to the House Select Committee on Post-War Military Policy, June 11, 1945 to reveal the continuity of our testimony in Washington. Mr. Chairman, while registering our resolute convictions we want to affirm our goodwill toward the United States government and our desire to be loyal, useful citizens as we maintain our allegiance to the supreme law of Christian love.

Respectfully submitted,
MENNONITE CENTRAL COMMITTEE
Rev. P. C. Hiebert, Hillsboro, Kansas
Chairman, Mennonite Central Committee
Rev. Albert Gaeddert, Inman, Kansas
Acting chairman, Peace Section, Mennonite Central Committee
Rev. Amos Horst, Akron, Pennsylvania
Member, Peace Section, Mennonite Central Committee
Rev. Don E. Smucker, Chicago, Illinois
Member, Peace Section, Mennonite Central Committee
Rev. C. N. Hostetter, Grantham, Pennsylvania
Brethren in Christ Church
Ernest W. Lehman, Akron, Pennsylvania
Peace Section Staff, Mennonite Central Committee

Paul L. Goering, 941 Mass. Ave. NW, Washington 1, D.C.
Peace Section Staff, Mennonite Central Committee
March 31, 1948

Reading 6

The following is the text of a letter sent to President Lyndon B. Johnson by the Mennonite Central Committee on June 2, 1965.

PEACE IN VIETNAM

Akron, Pa. (MCC)--The Executive Committee of the Mennonite Central Committee met in Chicago on May 21, 1965, and decided to write you of our deep concern over the enlarging war in Vietnam with its consequent toll of human suffering. As you face this complex problem be assured of our prayers for the guidance and strength of God upon you as you discharge your heavy responsibilities.

For ten years the Mennonite Central Committee, the relief and service agency of the Mennonite churches of North America, has been engaged in programs of medical care, relief feeding, and family-child assistance in Vietnam. One of our relief workers has been a captive of the Vietcong for three years. The director of our overseas program returned three weeks ago from an administrative visit to Vietnam during which he reviewed our program there, including the medical services at Nhatrang and the food distribution which is conducted through the cooperation of the Vietnamese Protestant churches throughout South Vietnam. In recent days our director in Vietnam has investigated the possibilities of an enlarged medical service and relief program at Danang, Pleiku, and other areas in the coastal provinces where there are growing concentrations of refugees. In the next few months additional personnel will be sent to Vietnam to work in feeding stations, distribution of cloth, meat and other relief needs, and in mobile health care.

The program of International Voluntary Services has also been supported by Mennonite leaders and some of our young men are now active in the work in Vietnam. These men work with the village people and are very conscious of the real needs of the people. They would agree wholeheartedly with your words at Baltimore on April 7, "Neither independence nor human dignity will ever be won though by arms alone. It also requires the works of peace."

In the same speech you said that "now there must be a much more massive effort to improve the life of man in that conflict-torn corner of our world." That is one of the reasons we went to Vietnam and why we are increasing our help there. We urge you to proceed as soon as possible with the announced intentions for economic development programs for the people of that area under international auspices. We agree with you that "we cannot wait for peace to begin the job." In the operation of government aid and church related programs in South Vietnam we would hope that help would be given to the needy regardless of political considerations. Such a policy will help convince the peoples of Vietnam that our first interest is to help them meet their basic needs.

We share with you the conviction that "The guns and the bombs, the rockets and the warships, are all symbols of human failure." Let us then turn aside from them to the only way that can ultimately succeed, the way of peace.

We support you in pressing for a negotiated settlement, entering into unconditional discussions with whomever necessary to halt hostilities. We also concur with your observation that "This generation of the world must choose: destroy or build, kill or aid, hate or understand." It is difficult for us to make judgments of the best course to follow under specific circumstances because we do not have the information that is available only to you, our President. However, we are deeply convinced that an expanded war would not be in the interests of the American people in their relationship to the people of Asia, and we also believe that a cessation of bombing in North Vietnam should be an urgent objective of our government. We believe that an increase in economic and technical assistance may give you the opening that will lead to a negotiated settlement. Let us move in the direction of peace by an escalation of compassion rather than an escalation of conflict.

May God's blessing be upon you as you seek His will for peace and righteousness among the nations.

* * *

Mennonites and Alternative Service (CPS). The second most important accronym in the Mennonite vocabulary next to MCC was CPS. During World War II, nearly 5000 Mennonites served in Civilian Public Service in the United States. The story is told well in Melvin Gingerich, SERVICE FOR PEACE: A HISTORY OF MENNONITE CIVILIAN PUBLIC SERVICE. Akron: MCC, 1949., Pp. 508. The Canadian Mennonite story is told briefly in pages 412-424, but more fully in J. A. Toews, ALTERNATIVE SERVICE IN CANADA DURING WORLD WAR II. Winnipeg: Christian Press Ltd., 1959., Pp. 127. Since MCC was not involved in the Canadian program no further reference will be made to it here.

The CPS alternative to military service began in camps largely given to nature conservation, but later expanded to agricultural and hospital service. This experience for the churches and the individuals involved was pivotal with regard to relations with government, other churches, and indeed in launching the service ministries of the church, especially MCC, around the world.

Reading 7

Excerpt, Meeting Concerning Alternative Service Programs, MCC and Mennonite Central Peace Executive Committees, October 26, 1940, Newton, KS.

O. O. Miller who had been appointed on October 4th as M. C. P. C. representative on the Executive Committee of the National Council for Religious Objectors reported developments to date in the organization of the National Council's Washington office. In this connection he read minutes of the several National Council Executive Committee meetings. The tentative (Nov., Dec., Jan.) three months budget was also presented. After this followed discussion of plans for meeting the Mennonite share of this. This report and action of the National Council were approved.

M.C.C. Sec'y Miller then reported developments and plans on the Alternate Service problem and states what was envisioned by way of a central office in Washington for taking care of our Mennonite concerns in this problem. The Sec'y recommended, and it was approved (1) That the action of Oct. 22nd, Washington meeting of the National Board of Civilian Service as noted in its minutes is approved. It was also approved that the M.C.C. proceed as noted under II 5 O. O. Miller memo in same "That main projects be agricultural - Government to furnish tools, material, housing, subsistence, transportation, technical direction and supervision - Mennonite Central Committee administration, discipline, education." (2) That M.C.C. Constituencies provide an advance deposit to the M.C.C. Treasurer of $50.00 for every assignee to "Work of National Importance"--this to provide for this assignee's share of Church overhead and administration for his year's service. Each M.C.C. representative is to carry the responsibility for presenting this policy to his group and of coordinating the forwarding of the funds with the M.C.C. Treasury. (3) That arrangements be made for a director of M.C.C. work projects, who could also initially function as director of M.C.C. Agriculture Camp, No. 1 and that authorization be given for later appointment of three more camp directors. Secretary was authorized to recommend the first director to the committee by correspondence.

After considerable further discussion of policies which might be advocated to Mennonite draftees in the matter of receiving and using wage allowances for government work, it was decided by unanimous vote to advocate to the several constituencies through their M.C.C. representatives that any such donated draftee allowances be made available to the M.C.C.

for projects outlined in October 22nd Civilian Service Board minutes and others which may develop that require funds aside from overhead and administration.

In the matter of continued information which should be available to M.C.C. constituents, it was suggested that full relief information should be sent to all M.C.C. members and also to Jesse Hoover, Samuel Witmer, C. F. Klassen, and S. F. Coffman of the cooperating organizations and J. L. Horst Secretary of the Mennonite Relief Committee. It was further suggested that all information in regard to Alternate Service go to the foregoing and to members of the M.C.P.C. not included in the foregoing list. It was also suggested that minutes of all meetings of the Washington Council for Religious Objectors and of the National Civilian Service Board to M.C.C. and M.C.P.C. Executive committee members.

It was decided to ask Paul Comly French to prepare a brief statement of the C.O. viewpoint in connection with the present conscription act, which could be used as a press release in any communities desired. This statement should be approved by the National Council Executive Committee and should cover C.O. appeal case policies and outline policies of an alternate service program. Such release or releases should be made available to our ministry through our M.C.P.C. channels.

Approved to appropriate $100.00 to furnish literature for Canadian internees--this in response to C. F. Klassen's Oct. 1st. letter, the remittance to be sent to Bro. Klassen to be used as he sees fit.

Approved to recommend to the M.C.C. annual meeting in December that the continuing administration of the M.C.C.'s work project program in connection with the Conscription Act be by joint M.C.C. and M.C.P.C. Executive Committees.

* * *

The following reading interprets the MCC understanding of CPS for those in the church who felt, on the one hand, that CPS meant being co-opted by government, and on the other, by those who felt it was too ecumenical.

Reading 8

Statement of Policy, Mennonite Civilian Public Service, from Gingerich, SERVICE FOR PEACE, pp. 447-451.

Appendix 13
STATEMENT OF POLICY
MENNONITE CIVILIAN PUBLIC SERVICE

The Mennonite Central Committee serves as an administrative

agency for foreign relief work and Civilian Public Service for the various branches of the Mennonite Church in the United States and the affiliated denomination known as the Brethren in Christ. The Mennonite branches constitute a family of evangelical bodies (125,000 baptized members in the USA) with a common heritage of faith going back to the Swiss and Dutch Anabaptists of the Reformation period (1525), and constitute the oldest of the so-called "historic peace churches." From the very beginning of their history the Mennonites have been opposed to methods of violence and to participation in military service and war in any form, basing their position on the teachings of the New Testament, particularly the Sermon on the Mount. They have always held that the Christian must follow Christ completely in a life of love, peace, and nonresistance, believing that constructive nonresistance means overcoming evil with good. They have taught and practiced mutual aid within the Christian brotherhood, even as they have also sought to minister to the relief of the world's needy. They have sought to live and testify to a way of life from which the use of force and compulsion is completely eliminated, whether in international, class, or personal relations, and is replaced by a creative expression of love and spiritual power which follows from the experience of regeneration and discipleship through faith in Jesus Christ and the possession of the indwelling Spirit of God. They have sought the solution of concrete social and economic problems in the application of the principles derived from the teachings of the Bible, and have viewed the church as a universal Christian brotherhood in which Christ is Lord and to which all men should be invited.

In their practice of Christian love and brotherhood, the Mennonites have always insisted that the approach to problems of human need, and the procedure to be used, be nonpolitical, and that all commitments be voluntary and personal. They were the first Christian group to advocate freedom of conscience and complete separation of church and state. They have also generally refused all participation in political and executive functions of the state, since these functions are based ultimately on the sanction of force and include the administration of national and local armed forces (including the police) which involves coercion and the taking of human life.

From the above description it is clear why the Mennonites do not consider themselves "pacifists" in the accepted modern sense of the term, since these groups frequently base their philosophy and action programs on humanitarian or general moral and religious considerations, rather than exclusively on the New Testament, and since they often resort to political activity and pressure in their efforts to attain their objectives.

Relation to Government in Civilian Public Service

Mennonites hold that it is the Christian's duty loyally and faithfully to obey the state in all requirements which do not involve violation of the Christian conscience, that is, a violation of the teachings of the Word of God. They assuredly believe a Christian must obey God rather than man when the demands of the State conflict with this supreme loyalty to Christ, but they also hold that the Christian should "Render unto Caesar the things that are Caesar's," and "Obey every ordinance of man for the Lord's sake." Although they acknowledge that it is within the province of the state to require service of its citizens, they reserve the right to refuse such service if it is contrary to conscience. This attitude toward state service does not constitute an endorsement of conscription or compulsion as such, but is rather an expression of the principle of obedience to the powers that be.

In like manner, the Mennonite Central Committee takes a positive rather than a merely negative attitude toward the Selective Service Administration and other government agencies which are responsible by law and presidential directive for the administration of this state service. It co-operates with Selective Service as far as it can in the development and administration of concrete programs of service, and recognizes the ultimate jurisdiction and power of this agency to determine the terms and conditions of service such as location and type of work, hours, pay, etc. It reserves the right of conscience to reject forms of service which contribute to war or coercion in any form or to any other social evil. It makes no claim for compensation either for the man working or for itself, although it does not consider it wrong to receive such compensation provided no compromising commitment to government policies is involved.

The Mennonite Central Committee holds, however, that government control of men in service should apply only to the work and working time, and to such matters as furloughs and leaves from the place of assigned duty. The nature and amount of after-work activities, and the character of the life of the men during their leisure time, should be the exclusive province of the responsible administrative agency (in this case the M.C.C.) in co-operation with the working men. The M.C.C. does, however, recognize the right of Selective Service to inspect all the functions performed by the administrative agency relating to the health, safety, and welfare of the men, as well as all matters pertaining to the maintenance of sound relations with the government.

In view of this policy of co-operation between the government and church agencies in C.P.S., and in view of privileges this offers to the agencies and the men in their charge, the Mennonite Central Committee is willing to finance not only its own operation expenses but the support of the men under its administration in so far as the government does not provide maintenance for the latter, although it does hold that logically government maintenance is justified for men in state service.

The Mennonite Central Committee has accepted the obligation to provide for all Mennonite men in Civilian Public Service both administratively and financially. It conceives of its service principally as a service to the Mennonite churches and their men in C.P.S., and accordingly operates loyally in accord with the spirit and principles of these churches. Non-Mennonite men who wish to serve in M.C.C. administered units and who are ready to co-operate with this administration and accept its policies are heartily welcome to its camps and projects. They will be accepted up to the limits of M.C.C. administrative and financial capacity, with the understanding that they or their constituencies contribute to their own support as much as possible.

The Mennonite Central Committee finances its work solely through voluntary contributions from its constituent bodies, and depends on each body to furnish the necessary funds for the support of its men and for the financing of its share of C.P.S. administration. Donations from non-Mennonite sources are accepted only as a contribution toward the support of non-Mennonite men.

Relation to Other C.P.S. Administrative Agencies

Accepting the requirement of Selective Service that one representative office be set up through which the C.P.S. administrative agencies shall deal with S.S. as a unit, the Mennonite Central Committee has participated in the setting up, operation, and financial support of the National Service Board for Religious Objectors. It recognizes this Board as the servant of the C.P.S. administrative agencies and as the proper place to review and co-ordinate such common or joint policies as are necessary in C.P.S. It does not consider the N.S.B.R.O. to have any jurisdiction in the administration of C.P.S. or in the formulation or operation of policies governing the life of the men under the administraion of the M.C.C. The M.C.C. is happy to note the advantageous functioning of the N.S.B.R.O. and the relation of mutual respect and confidence which has obtained among the administrative agencies represented on the N.S.B.R.O. However, its participation in the N.S.B.R.O. is not to be construed as necessarily signifying agreement with the other agencies or members of the N.S.B.R.O. in points of social or religious philosophy or administrative policy. The M.C.C. appreciates the valuable services rendered by the N.S.B.R.O. and is glad to contribute its proportionate share of the cost of its operations.

M.C.C. Policies in the Administration of C.P.S. Camps and Projects

Since Mennonites hold nonparticipation in war and violence, as well as constructive service to the state, to be an essential expression of Christian discipleship, the Mennonite Central Committee considers that the men who choose its C.P.S. camps, do declare by that act their intention to live in the spirit of Christian brotherhood during their C.P.S. service. Consequently, it organizes and administers C.P.S. camps and projects as Christian communities in which fellowship and worship, the preaching of the Gospel, the studying of the Word of God, and earnest Christian living are normal and basic experiences. It holds that the same high standard of Christian living must be expected in C.P.S. as is expected in the home community, church, and family. It accordingly assumes responsibility for a Christian pastoral ministry and for the cultivation and maintenance of Christian ethical standards among the men under its administration, as well as for the provision of a profitable and enriching Christian educational and recreational program.

As an administrative agency responsible both to its own Mennonite constituent bodies and Selective Service, the M.C.C. assumes responsibility for the total administration of the camps and projects assigned to it, and for the men who have chosen to accept its administration, and exercises this responsibility through an executive staff in each camp or project, appointed by it and responsible solely to it. While retaining ultimate responsibility and authority, the M.C.C. holds that participation in the life of a Christian brotherhood community such as it seeks to maintain in C.P.S. projects, in the truest sense means sharing by all members not only in the benefits, but in the creation of these benefits through mutual counsel and the bearing of burdens. It holds that true Christian brotherhood requires the democratic and Christian consideration of the needs of all, and the enlistment of the abilities and capacities of all for the common good, although the lines of administrative responsibility in actual procedures must still be clearly understood and respected.

The M.C.C. holds that it is the obligation of the men in C.P.S. to accept, within the limits of conscience and physical capacity, the work assignments made by Selective Service and the government technical agencies who supervise the work projects, both as to type and location of work, and as to individual duties, although this acceptance in every case is conditioned upon an assurance that the work involves no material contribution to the war effort and no violation of the Christian conscience in any way. Since this assurance is best secured by participation in the choice of work, the M.C.C. co-operates with Selective Service in the selection of work projects, and recommends to the men under its administration only such projects which it has approved.

The M.C.C. holds further that once a work assignment has been accepted it should be performed with the highest efficiency and dispatch and with a whole heart, for the Christian should always serve and work not "with eyeservice as a manpleaser but in singleness of heart, fearing the Lord." It considers work with the soil and natural resources of the nation, both plant and animal, to be an important service wholly worthy of acceptance by men in C.P.S., although forms of service which minister to human material and spiritual needs frequently are more urgent and valuable, particularly in times of emergency and exceptional need such as war and disaster. It also considers ministry to the needs of men and communities in foreign lands, whether in the form of relief or reconstruction work for the victims of war, or ministry to purely peacetime needs, to be thoroughly desirable and justifiable forms of service for C.P.S. men. It actively co-operates with Selective Service in seeking to discover and organize work projects consistent with the above principles.

The Meaning and Significance of C.P.S.

Mennonites consider Civilian Public Service to be significant and valuable, not only to the nation, but to the men in service, and to the Mennonite groups who finance and administer C.P.S. through the M.C.C.

C.P.S. work is valuable to the nation not only because of the direct achievement of the work projects, whether in soil conservation, forestry, reclamation, farm service, mental hospital service, etc., but also because of the demonstration of good teamwork and a high sense of devotion to the welfare of the community and the nation as a whole, or even of foreign communities.

C.P.S. work has meaning to the men who perform it as an expression of loyalty and love to their country, and of their desire to make a contribution to its welfare. It has still larger meaning as constructive service and ministry to human needs, and as a demonstration of a way of life in peace and love in contrast to the destructiveness of war and violence.

To the Mennonite constituent groups who support C.P.S. work by finances and participation in C.P.S. administration, the program of C.P.S. becomes a testimony for the way of life which they hold to be Christ's way, a way of peace and love and ministering to human needs which they hold to be a divine imperative. They desire to transform the compulsion of C.P.S. into the free service of a Christian who seeks to establish the kingdom of God among men by the preaching of the Gospel and the practice of Christian discipleship.

This statement of policy was approved at the Mennonite Central Committee Executive Committee Meeting on September 16, 1943.

CPS BULLETIN
A Weekly Publication of Mennonite Civilian Public Service
March 25, 1947 Vol. VI, No. 14

BIRD'S-EYE VIEW OF CPS

The life span of Civilian Public Service fell short one month of reaching six years. In May, 1941, the first of a total of over 12,000 young men entered CPS to do work of national importance as an alternative to entering the carnage of war that was carried on by the armed forces of the world. During the ensuing years, this group of 12,000 men served in 152 different base camps, units and special projects. Base camps made up 62 of the total number of projects. Of these base camps 58 were administered mainly by the three Historic Peace Churches--Mennonite, Church of the Brethren and the Society of Friends. The remaining four camps were administered by the government; five of the 58 church-operated camps later transferred to government administration.

The Mennonite Central Committee operated 66 of the total number of base camps, units and special projects. Of the 12,000 men in all CPS, approximately 5,830 participated in MCC operated camps with the largest number of men in camp at any given time reaching 4,288 in September of 1945. In order to operate this large number of camps it was necessary to recruit 192 directors and assistant directors and 242 educational directors. It cost $3,155,000 to finance this program and this large sum was obtained entirely through the voluntary contributions of the Mennonite and Brethren in Christ churches.

Is the Civilian Public Service all over now? From the point of government regulation we are all happy that it is, but the spirit of service should never end within us. Unless a spirit of service to our fellow man continues to control our thinking, a large part of our testimony given through CPS will have been lost. I just now recall what a preacher of another denomination told the CPS men at Henry, Illinois, in the beginning of the CPS program. He said, "You have now attracted our attention, but what we are going to watch is, what are you going to do after this is over to prove that you have something." Someone has rightfully said, "The debts we owe to God are payable to man." The opportunity is now ours to exhibit this spirit of service.

BENEDICTION

"The grace of the Lord Jesus Christ, and the love of God, and the communion of the Holy Ghost, be with you all. Amen." (II Cor. 13:14)

* * *

The following Reading reflects the pastoral concern of the church and MCC for the Mennonite men, and sometimes their wives, who lived in this conscripted situation. Alternative Service, when it returned in 1951, was much decentralized as individual conscientious objectors frequently found an assignment on their own. MCC again was given the mandate to establish units utilizing objectors in service assignments and pastoral services to those not in a church sponsored position.

Reading 9

August 30, 1945 letter from P. C. Hiebert, Chairman of MCC.

A Personal Message to All Men in C.P.S.

Dear friends and brethren in Christ:

May grace and peace abide with you ever.

By proclamation of the President of the United States, hostilities between the warring nations have been ordered to cease. At this news all our hearts rejoice and we feel as though we were relieved of the burden of sympathetic suffering occasioned by the horrors of the World War. All of us should halt and praise the Lord not only for ending the hostilities but also for His grace and love which has so wonderfully carried us through this emergency and at all times provided for our needs.

Your lives for the past years have been a living witness against the crime of war and for peace and the Jesus Way of life, which alone will satisfy the needs and deepest desires of humanity. This your service has value before God and man and should not cease with the announcement of the armistice, nor with your discharge from public service. As Mennonite Central Committee officials representing our churches and our constituency, we wish to express our appreciation of your heroic stand against public opinion and the forces that are in control.

Today I plan to admonish you to GET READY TO GO HOME! Getting ready to go home, however, includes much more than the packing of your suitcases and the purchase of your transportation. It means in addition to prepare to get yourself back into civilian life and into a society which is not what you left some years ago. It has changed, and you also have changed, probably to a much greater extent than you yourself realize. As a friend and one who is deeply concerned not only in your welfare but also in your witness for the better way of life, I feel led this afternoon to outline to you a few points that should be involved in your preparation for a safe and advantageous return to civilian life.

1. Check to see whether you have grown in the Christian graces--in faith, in the strength of your conviction, and in loyalty to God and the Church during your stay in Civilian Public Service.

2. Orient yourself intellectually to be prepared to give reason for the stand that you have taken at a considerable sacrifice, for to return without being prepared to defend your stand would be embarrassing to you as well as to your friends and supporters.

3. Formulate your convictions in words, and it may be well to put them on paper, and then get ready to stand by them with meekness and firmness, continuing in the fear of the Lord during your days of liberty as well as during your days of service.

4. Endeavor to stabilize yourself emotionally so that you are prepared to meet misinterpretations of your stand and unavoidable opposition and criticisms that you may face when you again will mingle freely with others who have had experiences during these years very different from those that were yours. You will find an indifferent if not a hostile world; nevertheless, be not afraid, but trustfully humble, and strong.

5. This world is much in need of your testimony of peace even though it be unpopular. Now is the time to let your light shine even though men love darkness rather than light. Remember that your light shines farthest when the night is darkest. Let us look to Christ, the beginner and finisher of our faith, who steadfastly set his face to go to Jerusalem when He knew that He would there be crucified.

6. Prepare to find and meet ideals of life among your friends far different from what you expect. Do not pose as a martyr, neither anticipate to be on the receiving end, but rather gather fortitude to return as a contributor in understanding, in consecration to the religion of Christ and in the service of your fellowmen in and through your church and your former circle of friends.

We trust that neither your patience nor endurance may be overtaxed during the period of delay which is bound to follow the announcement of the armistice, but rather that you would improve your time to leave behind a record of good and faithful service, a clear witness, and an evidence that you have profited by your experiences. May your service be the best and your witness the clearest and truest while you GET READY TO GO HOME.

Reading 10

Evaluation of the first five years of I-W service, which finally ended when the draft ended in 1974. Findings of I-W Evaluation and Planning Conference, April 9-10, 1957.

Factual Background

Almost five years ago, on July 1, 1952, the present alternative service program for conscientious objectors to military service in the United States had its beginning. Two years ago the decentralization of our sponsorship of the I-W program began. The purpose of this meeting is to evaluate the entire program in terms of its satisfactoriness to the Mennonite Church (MC) as an alternative to military service, and also to consider together possible improvements in the sponsorship plans of the various conferences.

The facts which we face include the following:

1. The program seems to be satisfactory to the government. The plan works smoothly, the service record of the men is good. Human resources are being used to useful purposes, and the plan costs the government nothing.

2. There is little or no opposition from the general citizenry.

3. Local boards have usually been cooperative, and Selective Service has maintained the right of men to volunteer for service in any approved agency of their choice.

4. The present alternative system seems likely to continue as long as the draft continues.

5. Selective Service has approved 1700 agencies for I-W service, in almost every state and territory, and in 41 countries.

6. In the first four years 6500 I-W's have been assigned, roughly a third of them, more than 2000, belonging to the Mennonite Church. There are now 700 of our men in service.

7. Most of our men (more than 85% have volunteered before their induction date. The proportion of men serving in church-sponsored projects including PAX service abroad, has increased from 10% at the beginning of the program to 30% at the present time.

8. The age of our I-W's, about 19½ at the beginning of service, is lower than that of military draftees, between 22 and 23.

9. A strong stand for the ideal of voluntary service was taken by General Conference in 1949, when there was no draft. The Peace Problems Committee has urged voluntary service for many years. This service attitude has furnished

a good foundation for the alternative service program.

10. It was decided at the beginning that there should be no over-all Mennonite Central Committee administration of I-W as there was for C.P.S.

11. Since this administration was to be denominational, the Peace Problems Committee has carried and still carries general responsibiltiy for the helpful functioning of the I-W program.

12. Central coordination was early assigned to the Relief and Service Committee by the Peace Problems Committee. Pastoral services and other services were to be integrated.

13. Later central administration was changed to decentralized sponsorship by conferences and congregations. But the Relief and Service Committee, together with Mennonite Central Committee, still furnishes over-all coordination.

14. Teaching and orientation have included these methods: week-end I-W conferences, congregational and regional; a quarter of Sunday-school lessons; an annual registration of 16-year-olds, which give a list for a series of mailings of material provided by Relief and Service Committee; orientation schools by Mennonite Central Committee; orientation retreats; church-wide and district nonresistance conferences; sermons on Peace Sunday; Mennonite Youth Fellowship discussions; production of peace literature.

15. At various I-W centers fellowships have developed, with congregations growing out of them; as at Roseburg (Ore.), Indianapolis, and Cleveland.

16. The ration of men asking for I-W classification (about 90%) is much higher than during World War II.

Evaluation

Although we do not favor the principle of conscription, we are grateful to the government for the privilege of alternative service. We appreciate the type of government administration now in effect, and feel the government is doing a good job in achieving its purposes: the effective use of the I-O man-power pool for human welfare.

For the church also the I-W work program is serving well enough that we have no better system to suggest. It drives us to service that we ought as Christians to perform. It calls our young men to individual responsibility that can make for growth in character and Christian experience. It is discovering and developing leadership which the church can use. It gives the church a larger world perspective and greatly extends our Christian testimony. It opens up vocational opportunities for our young people.

As compared with C.P.S., I-W has its limitations. Group life is less evident. Individualism is more noticeable. However, there is less griping and frustration. The men do not feel so helpless and dependent on the church for financial support. They are just as free to talk to ministers as were the C.P.S. men. They are just as glad for visits from friends and pastors. It is too soon to feel the total impact from I-W, but there is reason to feel that it is serving the church well today.

We must remember that I-W was set up by the government for its ends, not for the spiritual ends of witness and service. It has been our task to transform the draft into Christian opportunity and accomplishment. We are less satisfied than is the government with the results. But the failure belongs to us, and not to the system. Two thousand I-W men, each serving two years, have a potential of four thousand years of Christian witness. This potential is far from being realized. But the fault is not inherent in the system.

We do labor under disadvantages in I-W. Since it is easy to secure I-O classification, and since there is little opposition or persecution, I-W service may actually neutralize peace convictions. Men not prepared for the experience can be overwhelmed by new situations and overcome by temptations. Urbanization and breaking of community is accelerated, and many men are not returning to the home community. Some marry outside the church. Some are being lost to the church, temporarily or permanently. There is a strong tendency to make the experience only two years "put in" for Selective Service and "set free" from home and church.

The spirit of independence is a leading problem. The system permits men to choose their own employment and the time for beginning I-W assignment. They may make their own living arrangements. They may or may not participate in unit life. They attend religious services only when they want to. No one but themselves controls their use of leisure time and the way they spend their wages. Immature youth, away from home for the first time, are often unable to use wisely this new freedom.

One of the strengths of the system is the greater use of personal responsibility. But men unprepared and unequipped spiritually cannot use this greater freedom. This is therefore probably the greatest danger of the I-W system. Here is a paradox which cannot be avoided. Our men must be treated as adults, but the system breaks down if they lack the inner discipline of Christian character.

The outcomes of the plan, good or bad, reveal the real quality of our church and home life. Here is a mirror by which we may judge ourselves. As our sons succeed or fail, they reveal our spiritual vitality or weakness.

Our experience in administering I-W so far reveals:

1. Men do best when some home and church connections are maintained. The sense of belonging must be kept unbroken

so far as possible. Pastoral contacts, church bulletins, and visits help. Failures often come from poor communication.

2. The need to maintain home contact requires thoughtful direction, however. It is important that I-W men be encouraged to enter fully into the Christian fellowship of a congregation or the I-W unit at their place of service. In many, if not most communities, coming home too often may interfere with the witness. Families should visit their men sometimes rather than encourage them to come home too often.

3. While church-related service is best, we are happy for earning too. The wide variety of job opportunities and financial arrangements in earning service has been a good thing. But if earning service is chosen, older or married men generally contribute more and fare better than younger or single men.

4. In VS and Pax the man enters service through the church and continues service in it. Such service is superior in evangelistic and church building possibilities.

5. We should not, however, expect too much of I-W service. The youth of the men, their short period of residence, and their irregular hours of work often hinder an effective contribution in church building.

6. The provision for orientation of our men is often inadequate. For the great change into the I-W situation, and then again back into the home church, more guidance is necessary. Home and congregation also need to be helped to understanding and full cooperation. The system, however, does not allow for compulsory orientation. It must be effectively and attractively offered as a help.

7. Decentralization of sponsorship seems to be sound in principle. It gives a greater sense of responsibility to a larger group of people. It ties I-W service more closely into the life of the church. It fits into the decentralization of Selective Service administration. What has been lost in simplicity of administration has been offset by psychological advantages. Excellent work has been done by some sponsoring groups and persons. Where sponsoring is inadequate, it can be improved. Probably we have been asking too much of our sponsors who usually have only marginal time.

8. There are some missing links in our procedures for getting information about the who, where, when, and what of I-W movements. We owe it to our sponsors to get more information to them. They frequently know too little about the men who are their responsibility, and they know it too late.

Looking Ahead

1. If the I-W program is not to be a hazard to the life and work of the church, and if it is to rise to something nearer its potential, it requires more careful study.

The program must be analyzed and better answers must be found. This should be assigned to an individual with time and ability to present recommendations to the church.

2. Such conferences as this one, or smaller conferences on an area level, should be repeated. Administrators and sponsors need direction and stimulation.

3. We must constantly evaluate our peace position to give it relevancy to the world situation and to current thinking.

4. We must strengthen our teaching program. Our nonresistance must not be an emergency position for certain persons at certain times, but must be thoroughly integrated into the Christian faith of all our people. We must find new and more effective ways to do this.

5. We need to relate I-W more closely to our whole youth program. I-W men must think of themselves and be thought of not as a special class, but in the context of our whole church life. Support of a full-time youth secretary may be a means to this end.

6. Sponsorship must be strengthened. Over-all administration must see that continuity is maintained and that gaps are filled. Sponsors with a conviction for the task and time to devote to it must be chosen. Laymen might be used more widely. Sponsors should be given necessary financial support. They should be helped to clearly defined objectives for their contacts with I-W men.

7. Orientation procedures must be improved. The subject matter must be broad enough to include matters of faith and conduct. The persons to be served must include men, parents, girl friends and wives; in fact, the whole congregation. Conferences and sponsors carry this responsibility, but the Peace Problems Committee and the Relief and Service Committee can give guidance. Released I-W men should be able to give help here.

8. Preparation for service involves our homes and families. Here our young men must experience Christian love to the full in order that they may be ready to move out into service. When the time for I-W service comes, it should come as one more expression of love, rooted in Christian experience with God and fellowmen.

9. Any confusion in Mennonite church relations with Mennonite Central Committee in I-W work should be clarified. Our sponsor-pastors should be sensitive to needs of I-W men from other Mennonite groups, ministering to their spiritual needs in a gracious manner, without neglecting their loyalty to their own church groups.

10. The church should send qualified couples into areas where I-W men are employed to help to build Christian fellowship and witness around their home life.

11. We must continue to promote the principles of church related service irrespective of the draft. We echo the statement of General Council of General Conference of 1949: "We believe that all those who would follow Christ in full discipleship in the way of peace and love are at all times called to serve the needs of the world both spiritual and material in the name and spirit of Christ. Since the distresses and needs of our world are so insistent and constant, the General Council calls upon our churches and particularly our young men and women, to a new sense of divine calling. . . All our young people should seriously face the question before God, whether they should now offer themselves for a substantial period of direct Christian service." Young women, released I-W's, undrafted men, and older people have as great an obligation in Christian service as do our drafted men. As Selective Service tends to increase the age at which men are being called, we recognize the temptation to avoid service completely. We believe this to be out of harmony with true Christian commitment.

12. We need to study the types of projects in which the I-W men are giving their service, as to their positive contributions, their creativeness with regard to personality development and expression, their evangelistic and witness opportunities, their adaptability to voluntary service possibilities.

13. Since our failures in I-W are primarily spiritual, we must strengthen the foundations of our religious life. We must develop loyalty to Christ, not only to a culture or a tradition. Our people must have a faith which can flourish in any environment. If I-W is to be fruitful, we must grow young men who can stand on their own feet. We must find ways through the work of the Spirit among us to strengthen the vitality of faith in home and congregation. We must strengthen the spirit of fellowship in our home churches, that love may be in deed as well as in creed. All of our people, including our young men, must be brought to a full commitment to Christ and the Gospel, with all that that involves. At the heart of all our I-W work lies the Christian experience of the I-W man.

* * *

War Bonds and War Taxes. It is not easy for an individual to say no to social and political pressures which appeal for solidarity in the face of military actions. It is ever so much more difficult for a person to decide how to use his/her resources for just and righteous causes. Mennonites have frequently asked whether they could pay for war if they had a conscience against fighting a war. During World War I and II the major issue was the enormous public pressure to buy bonds to pay for the war. The following Reading reports to Mennonite pastors the provision for Civilian Bonds which presumably would be used for non-military purposes. The year of the letter was 1942.

Reading 11

MENNONITE CENTRAL COMMITTEE
PEACE SECTION
Akron, Pennsylvania

To all Pastors of M.C.C. Constituencies:

Provision has at last been made for subscription to Civilian Bonds in lieu of Defense or War Bonds. We have prayed and striven for this during the past months. Today our hope has been realized. We can now offer our people subscriptions to Government Bonds that are not for war purposes, with provision also made for recognition of such subscriptions. This opens up an avenue of service for which many of our people have long been pressing, as evidenced by the many anxious inquiries that have come to us during the past months, wondering whether we could not offer some solution to the growing pressure for purchase of Defense or War Bonds.

Although this plan is not all that might have been hoped and expected, and it may be open to certain criticisms, yet we are grateful for the provision made available to us.

After having tried without success to work out other methods of procedure, we have now adoped the plan as described in the enclosed folder. In short, the Provident Trust Company of Philadelphia has agreed to act as fiscal agent in subscribing to bonds from the Treasury Department when suitable issues are available. A Bond Committee, composed of a representative from each of the three historic Peace Church groups, will decide upon specific subscriptions to available current offerings. The bonds will be duly registered by the Treasury Department and then forwarded to subscribers, or to those for whom subscribers have had them registered.

There may be some question concerning the reason for a fiscal agent as intermediary with the Government. In seeking to work out other plans we found that it would probably require at least a year to obtain all necessary permits and similar details for setting up a private corporation for handling bonds; but perhaps the greatest obstacle of all was the tax situation. We were driven to conclude that such a plan was not feasible.

At the meeting of leaders of our several church groups held in Chicago, June 25, details of the present plan were presented. It was unanimously agreed by all groups represented that we should go ahead with this as the only available plan at present open to us. The responsibility for its further operation, so far as the Mennonites and associated groups are concerned, was given over to the M.C.C., which in turn referred it to the Peace Section. Orie O. Miller is the M.C.C. representative on the Bond Committee.

Enclosed with this letter you will find a supply of a descriptive circular which gives full details of the operation of the program. This was prepared by the Civilian Bond Committee and the Provident Trust Company, with the approval of the Treasury Department. We believe that it needs little or no explanation. An individual so desiring may purchase a bond for himself alone, or jointly with another person, or in the name of another person or institution. By way of example in the latter case: One may wish to contribute to a church institution. The order form should be filled out with the name of the institution as the party for whom the bond is to be registered. The purchaser will receive a receipt for the subscription, and his local community or county will receive credit on its bond quota. The bond, when completed, will be sent to the institution for which purchased and registered. At the maturity of the bond, the institution will receive its cash value. The receipt sent to the subscriber will also furnish evidence for income tax deductions.

Enclosed is also a supply of a subscription order form. When filled out this is to be sent to the Provident Trust Company with the proper amount of money to cover the bond purchase. We especially emphasize the necessity for applicants to complete all the details requested in this form. Omission of any part of the information will make impossible the proper functioning of our program. Will you please emphasize to your people the necessity for filling in the forms so they are complete in every detail?

Both the descriptive circulars and the order forms are furnished on the basis of 20% of your recorded membership. It is our purpose to get this information into the hands of every family in our M.C.C. constituency. More are available at the Mennonite Central Committee office if needed.

Subscription orders may be sent directly to the Provident Trust Company, Philadelphia, Pennsylvania, or they may be forwarded through the local soliciting agent. The question has been raised as to whether the subscriptions might be given to the Defense Bond solicitor. This we feel would be satisfactory and perhaps desirable, if properly safeguarded. A receipt should always be held for all subscriptions, with evidence of the Civilian intention of such subscription. The Provident Trust Company is the sole fiscal agent for this alternate bond transaction, as at present set up, and subscriptions should be made on the official Subscription Order Forms.

Many of our people are working in factories or other

industrial establishments which have set up a pay roll allotment plan. The institution is desirious of meeting a certain quota. Instructions may be given to such institutions to hold in trust the usual percentage of the pay roll until sufficient funds have accumulated to subscribe to a bond. Instructions should be given them to subscribe through the Provident Trust Company to a Civilian Bond as designated by the Civilian Bond Committee, when sufficient funds have accumulated.

When using the Pay Roll Allotment, it is quite simple to strike out the words on the regular Government form, "United States Series E Savings Bonds," and substitute the words, "Civilian Government Bonds." The last paragraph should read: "This allotment is made in accordance with the terms and conditions of the plan agreed upon by the Treasury Department, the Civilian Bond Committee, and the Provident Trust Company for the purchase of Civilian Government Bonds."

There will undoubtedly be many individuals who will wish to subscribe for bonds but who do not have sufficient funds for such a bond in one lump sum. To relieve pressure for purchase of Defense or War Bonds as well as to make available this type of service to the smaller depositor, we suggest that each local congregation or district set up its own machinery for immediately receiving deposits toward bond purchases. A local bond committee might be set up as custodian of the funds. Or the regular church treasurer might serve this interest if so desired. To assist in the carrying on of such a program we have prepared (1) deposit forms for the use of the treasurer or trustee of local groups and (2) receipt forms to be used by such treasurer for recognition of deposits of individual subscribers. All this will serve as evidence to solicitors for War Bonds. A sample of each of these forms is also enclosed. When sufficient funds have been deposited with the local treasurer for the purchase of a bond, he should consult with the depositor about the details of subscribing for a bond--determining how it is to be registered, etc. This is designed, of course, for those who prefer to reserve funds for the individual purchase of a Bond. Other plans might also be used. A number of individuals might combine their funds for the purchase of a Bond, to be held in trust in the name of one of the depositors or some other officially designated person. Or it might be subscribed by the Church organization in the name of its officals, to be held in trust by them. The receipt forms could be used in either case to give proper recognition for such deposits.

A sample is also enclosed of a pledge form which some of our people have asked us to furnish. Some communities will find it useful in more effectively and immediately meeting pressure for purchase of War Bonds, to submit such pledge to the local solicitor. If you need a supply of these pledge, receipt or filing forms, please write to the Mennonite Central Committee, Akron, Pennsylvania. A small donation enclosed with your order to help defray costs of printing and mailing will be appreciated.

Yours in fellowship,
Orie O. Miller, Executive Secretary
Jesse W. Hoover, Peace Section Secretary

* * *

The dilemma of separating civilian bonds from war bonds is underscored by the following correspondence, which must not have been very encouraging to the Historic Peace Churches.

Reading 12

Excerpt, Letter of October 12, 1943 from Under Secretary of the Treasury A. W. Bell to Congressman Robert A. Grant.

Reference is made to your letter of October 1, enclosing a letter from Mr. Eli D. Miller, R.R. #1, Box 226, Middlebury, Indiana, who inquires concerning the United States Savings Bonds of Series F and G, which are being offered through the Provident Trust Company of Philadelphia.

The Treasury does not issue any bonds or other securities, the proceeds of which are earmarked for specific purposes. Amounts received by the Treasury for all issues of public debt obligations are paid into the general fund from which all expenditures of the Government are made, including both expenditures for direct war purposes and expenditures for other functions of the Government. It is not possible, therefore, to segregate funds obtained by the Treasury in the sale of public debt obligations according to the purposes for which such funds will be expended....

Sometime ago the National Service Board for Religious Objectors, 941 Massachusetts Avenue, N.W., Washington, D.C., made arrangements under which persons could subscribe through that organization for Treasury securities which do not bear any designation indicating that they are "War" bonds. Under the arrangements made, the National Service Board designated a fiscal agent, the Provident Trust Company of Philadelphia, for the purpose of accepting subscriptions from the members of the various groups represented by the National Service Board for the purchase of securities other than "War" bonds. We understand that the subscriber is required to pay the fiscal agent $1.00 for each subscription as a service charge. The fiscal agent on behalf of the various individuals who have subscribed for bonds, enters such subscriptions with the Treasury for Savings Bonds or market as and when offered, and only this is the organization referred to in your correspondent's letter. Such securities are issued in strict accordance with the terms of the circulars offering the various issues for subscription, and, of course, are no different in any respect from any other such securities which are sold in connection with the particular offering.

* * *

During the 1960's and 70's more and more Mennonites questioned the advisability of paying income taxes and the telephone excise tax designated for the Vietnam War. MCC Peace Section made itself available as a resource for persons with a conscience on war taxes.

Reading 13

TAXES FOR MILITARY PURPOSES. A Statement Adopted by the MCC Peace Section, November 15, 1975.

TAXES FOR MILITARY PURPOSES

As a Mennonite and Brethren in Christ people we have affirmed that our highest loyalty is to Jesus Christ and His kingdom. We have seen the way of peace as an integral part of the good news of salvation and have attempted to link our evangelistic witness and our nonresistant way of life. While we have often failed to live fully the way of love for the enemy which Jesus taught and have sometimes hidden our witness, we have agreed that this way does not permit us to participate in military service. Even where there have not been legal provisions allowing exemptions from or alternatives to military service we have generally felt called to obey God rather than man and have refused military service.

On the matter of taxes we have agreed on the legitimacy of taxation by governments and the obligation of Christians to pay taxes for all purposes which do not conflict with Christian conscience. The only such conflict which has been seriously dealt with among us is the payment of taxes for war.

We have not had clarity regarding payment of such taxes. As a community of faith we have not discerned the meaning of Jesus' words, "Render unto Caesar the things that are Caesar's, and unto God the things that are God's," as it applies to war taxes.

Generally we have not hesitated to pay taxes, even though some of the money collected has been used for military purposes. Taxes clearly identified as war taxes, however, have often not been paid by our forebears because of their desire to avoid participation in bloodshed.

In recent years the issue of taxes for military purposes

has again become a matter of serious concern for many sisters and brothers in the United States. While no taxes are collected specifically for war, we know that over half our tax money is used to pay for past wars, for current military expenditures and for preparation for future wars. We know that our participation in warfare through payment of federal taxes is increasing because we pay more taxes as many of us move away from the tradition of simple living which is our heritage. We know that the nature of modern warfare has changed and now relies much less on large numbers of soldiers and much more on highly sophisticated and expensive weapons. We know that war has become increasingly deadly and now threatens the very survival of the human race, and we know that the devastation of modern war can be unleashed with the direct personal participation of only a few.

We sense that our peace witness, expressed through our historic refusal to personally participate in the military, is made less effective as a result of this shift in the nature of warfare. Our traditional witness is further muted by the fact that the present suspension of inductions, for which we are grateful, removes the occasion at which American Mennonites for the last 35 years have most clearly spoken for the way of peace by choosing alternate service instead of the military.

The concern over taxes paid for military purposes has been further deepened by a growing consensus that our calling as Christian peacemakers is not only to avoid participating in the military, but to actively witness to the way of peace and against militarism. We do not wish to deceive ourselves into thinking that we can remain aloof from the militarism we abhor by refusing to go ourselves or even by refusing taxes. We would not absolve ourselves of responsibility to persons in a burning building simply because we had not set the fire. We would seek to sound the alarm and to put out the fire. So too we must sound the alarm about the evils of militarism and seek to combat this peril to humankind, working to turn the world, and especially our country, from its suicidal course. Our Christian concern for our neighbor demands no less. Our evangelistic witness is discredited if we remain silent in the face of so great an evil.

Some in our midst, recognizing the link between our affluence and the poverty in much of the world, and wishing to support neither injustice nor way by paying taxes for the military, voluntarily reduce their income or increase contributions in order to rebuke the idolatrous spirit of commercialism, withdraw support from militarism and channel resources to kingdom causes. A small but growing number of persons from our churches can no longer in good conscience voluntarily pay their full federal taxes, despite the illegality of such refusal. There are many others who pay such taxes under protest because of the contribution to war which payment represents and who desire a legal alternative permitting payment of taxes for nonmilitary purposes only.

In order to make possible payment of federal taxes in good conscience by those opposed to paying for war, legislation has been introduced in the House of Representatives which, if passed, would allow tax payment to go only for peacemaking and nonmilitary purposes. While this legislation, entitled the World Peace Tax Fund Bill, would not address directly the primary problem of misplaced national reliance on military force, it would follow the precedent of alternate service legislation in at least allowing those with conscience on the matter of participation in war to channel their tax dollars to other causes. Such alternative provisions could in fact contribute to a careful look at the priority of the military if enough people choose to channel their taxes through this fund and at the same time continue their efforts against excessive military spending.

On the basis of the above the Peace Section (U.S.) recommends:

1. That congregations and conference bodies, recognizing the need for discernment together in the community of faith on matters of Christian faithfulness, seriously study the issue of paying federal taxes used for military purposes, seeking to discern the will of God for us in this matter.

2. That Mennonites and Brethren in Christ support legislation permitting payment of taxes into a special fund which would not be used for war purposes.

3. That Mennonites and Brethren in Christ continue to work toward reduction of military spending, not resting content with special provisions exempting us from payment of taxes for military purposes.

4. That Mennonites and Brethren in Christ affirm and support those in our midst who feel compelled by Christian conscience to refuse payment of all or some federal tax because of the large percentage of such taxes used for military purposes.

5. That Mennonites and Brethren in Christ affirm and support those whose sense of stewardship and concern with military spending lead them to reduce income or substantially increase charitable contributions in order to reduce support for war and share more fully with the needy world.

6. That Mennonite and Brethren in Christ institutions study the conflict between their Christian obligations and their legal obligations in the collection of federal taxes, expecially when employees request that war taxes not be withheld from their wages, and that institutions be encouraged to honor such requests.

* * *

The MCC Peace Section Washington Office. During the 1960's a major concern of the Peace Section was the growing inter-relationships of the church within the political order. Consequently the Peace Section developed a study process on Christian witness to government which culminated in a study conference held in Chicago October 7-9, 1965. After this, the General Conference Mennonite Church and the Mennonite Church peace committees urged the opening of a liaison office in Washington, D.C. The following report was written by the Director of the office, Delton Franz, recording some of the major developments of the first five years.

Reading 14

The MCC Peace Section Washington Office: A Review. Minutes of MCC-PS, March 29-31, 1973.

"Much to our chagrin, we discovered (on May 18, 1967) that many Congressmen did not know us as well as we--and they--thought they did. If they didn't know our views on induction, how can they know what we think on scores of other questions? And if we didn't know what was going on in Washington affecting us on the conscription issue, what do we know about what is going on in scores of other areas affecting our concerns and interests. The gospel has its social implications and government today is so great and so pervasive that whatever it does on almost any question is bound to affect in some way the life of the church and what it is trying to do. Whether government policy helps or hinders the work of the church depends much on whether or not men in government "know Joseph," and on what their attitude toward him is." (Guy F. Hershberger, Feb. 28, 1968, Gospel Herald)

Conscience Against War: The Forerunner of a Washington Office

The MCC Peace Section Washington Office was opened in July, 1968. Peace Section considerations to open a Washington office began much earlier however. In various ways, Mennonite personnel on the staff of the National Service Board for Religious Objectors (NSBRO) served in a limited and unofficial way as a Mennonite presence in the Capitol.

Prior to the opening of the Peace Section's Washington Office, Peace Section appointees, serving as NSBRO directors included Elmer Neufeld ('51-'54), Edgar Metzler ('54-'56), and Harold Sherk ('58-'69). The principal service of these men was, of course, to monitor Selective Service regulations and to provide draft counseling services to the conscientious objector. Conferral with the legislative branch in the interest of keeping abreast of legislation related to military conscription in the Congress was also NSBRO work.

The strong financial and staff involvement of MCC Peace

Section in NSBRO through the years reflected the prominant place which conscription played in Mennonite concerns. The draft was the point at which our religious convictions most explicitly intersected with the decisions of federal government and perennially prompted the communication of our concerns in Washington. (This was perhaps most dramatically evidenced in 1948 and 1952 when Universal Military Training legislation came before Congress, generating thousands of letters and telegrams from Mennonites--undoubtedly more response than on any other single issue in our history.)

Nevertheless, the fact that Mennonite personnel serving with NSBRO were, from time to time asked to investigage other concerns such as immigration laws, and P. L. 480 (Food for Peace) guidelines, indicates that our vigilance in the nation's capital was not restricted only to draft matters.

An expression of this broadening concern is indicated in the minutes of the June 8, 1966, meeting of the Peace Section Executive Committee: "The Executive Secretary reviewed the many indications of the increased interest in a more articulate Mennonite witness to the state. Our traditional willingness to testify when our own interests were involved in relation to conscientious objection have led to suggestions that we should also be willing to testify when the rights of others are involved. Various study conferences of Peace Section constituent groups have expressed a growing concern that witness to the state should be a dimension of our service of Christian compassion. The MCC study conference in Washington in 1961 provided a first-hand exposure to the role of church agencies seeking to relate their Christian concern to government, the ethical dilemmas of political decision-making and the opportunities and problems of a Christian working for the federal government."

The process of deciding to expand the scope of our vigilance in the Capitol was a deliberate and carefully considered one. It is noteworthy that it was the action and stimulus of constituent bodies that led to the Peace Section's opening of the Washington Office, not vice versa. At the January 13, 1966, annual meeting of the Peace Section, action was taken approving a November 6, 1965, minute by the Peace and Social Concerns Committee of the Mennonite Church and a similar action of the Peace and Social Concerns Committee of the General Conference (of the same date). The MC action read: "Moved and approved that in view of the discussions of a Washington Office on an inter-Mennonite basis over the years, we urge General Council of Mennonite General Conference and Mennonite Central Committee seriously consider the establishment of such an office."

At a June 8, 1966, meeting, the Section appointed Dwight King, then a Mennonite student at Harvard Divinity School to undertake a feasibility study in Washington, D.C. during August of 1966. A Showalter Foundation grant was received for this feasibility study outlining the following objectives:

1. Investigate operation of church agencies in Washington, including: a) how they view their role, theologically and from the perspective of political science, b) methods and procedures in relating to government, c) methods and procedures in relating to their constituency, d) how government officials view their activities, e) results of their work, both in terms of government and their constituencies.

2. Propose possible alternatives for a Mennonite office in Washington in view of: a) various Mennonite interests in the nation's capital, b) possibilities of cooperative effort with other church groups, c) current Mennonite witness to the state in particular.

At the Peace Section's Annual Meeting on January 19, 1967, a minute was passed affirming in principle the Peace Section's intention of increased representation in Washington. It was not until a year later, however, that a decisive action was agreed upon for the opening of a Washington Office. At the annual meeting in January of 1968, the guidelines for the Washington Office were accepted (see attachment: "Report and Recommendation Concerning a Washington Office"). These guidelines have served as a valuable compass in keeping clear the direction and function of the office. It is to that function and the practical enactment of the Washington Office mandate that we now turn.

After four and 3/4 years, several general observations might be made regarding strengths and weaknesses of the Washington Office.

Staff: Of MCC's 759 in-service personnel, 3 are assigned to the Peace Section Washington office: a full time director, a research assistant assigned on a one-year intern basis (MCC V.S.), and a rotating one year secretary (MCC V.S.). The obvious advantage of V.S. personnel serving in the latter two assignments are in affording more young people an opportunity to share in this experience as well as to operate the office on a modest budget. The disadvantage is the constant turnover of staff which requires initiating new recruits to the assignments.

Priorities of the Office: The Office has been assigned six issue-areas by the Peace Section. Legislation and executive policy is monitored in the areas of (1) the draft (2) military spending vs. human needs (3) economic development of developing nations (4) domestic poverty (5) racial justice and (6) preservation of human freedoms and religious liberty.

While all these are areas that relate to the interests and work of the church, it is acknowledged that a limited staff cannot fully develop the specialization and expertise that might be desirable in each of these areas. The Washington Office has by now, however, established relationship with a broad spectrum of governmental and private agancies, enabling the Office to tap specialized information when needed. Within a two block radius of the Office, such offices as the following are accessible: Nat'l Council to Repeal the Draft, Washington Office on Africa, Friends Committee on Nat'l Legislation, Baptist Joint Committee on Public Affairs, Nat'l Council on Prevention of Alcoholism, House and Senate Office Bldgs., Library of Congress, etc., etc.

While the Office concentrates in six areas, a growing number of inquiries from constituents require researching issues outside the areas outlined. Inasmuch as the Office exists to service constituency requests, the tension between human limitations and the growing scope of constituent inquiries is increasingly real. Recent requests received for technical data included areas such as public health, low-income housing, and political prisoners in Vietnam, tax credits for families using parochial schools, and inquiries from college and graduate students seeking information on Mennonites.

Relating to the Constituency: (Guidelines - "The office shall provide facilitating services for the constituent groups") While the need to communicate the office's function to the constituency will continue, the office has clearly moved beyond the initial period to the substantial work of providing accurate information on national policy from the perspective of Christian concern. Though not preoccupied with measuring constituency criticism or approval of the office, two observations might be made: (1) The mail received in Akron and Washington reflecting disapproval has been much less than might have been expected. The criticism that has been expressed has focused on subject matter that is emotional and controversial within our society, e.g. the threat of communism and prayer in public schools. Attached to such correspondence one may find the literature of Billy James Hargis and Gerald L. K. Smith literature, with its inclusion in the Washington Memo encouraged. Reasoned criticisms and suggestions have also been made which have proven instructive and helpful. (2) A second measurement of constituency response to a Mennonite involvement in the decisions of government is reflected in the Church Member Profile, conducted by professors Leland Harder of AMBS /Associated Mennonite Biblical Seminaries/ and Howard Kaufman of Goshen College. Three questions may be cited:

(a) It is not the business of the church to try to influence the actions of government in regard to such issues as war and peace, race relations, poverty, etc.

25% agree   20% uncertain   56% disagree

(b) Church members should witness directly to the state (nation) by writing to legislators, testifying before legislative committees.

61% agree 30% uncertain 9% disagree

1) Seminars: Seminars to expose constituents to current issues and the inner workings of government have been conducted for 1,261 constituents during the first almost five years. The objective has been not merely to acquaint constituents with the decision-making process in government, but to examine the urgent problems of our time in light of Christian faith. What does it mean to be a Christian in relation to government in a 20th century democracy? Beyond binding up the wound of the victims of warfare, what is the church's responsibility to affect systems and structures of violence, oppression, and injustices?

In addition to the general exposure seminars, special interest seminars are also conducted to facilitate the work of the church in a variety of specific problem areas, e.g. seminars on "The Church and The Offender," Southern Africa, and the Seminar on Indian Americans. Student groups, both high school and college, are increasingly utilizing the office for on-location education ventures. The office has scheduled interterm sessions for student groups from EMC, Messiah, Bluffton, Bethel and Hesston.

2) Workshops in Constituent Churches: Speaking engagements and forums in local congregations and at district conferences also serve as a means of raising to consciousness the relationship of current affairs to Christian obedience as well as to acquaint our people with the services and functions of the Washington Office.

These encounters have underscored the importance of biblical-theological training as a resource in the Washington assignment. Our people (to their credit) are concerned that a venture of this kind have its roots in the soil of our biblical heritage as well as in a knowledge of political science. Our young people have a growing interest in world affairs. They must also be helped to relate this interest to Christian ethics and faith.

3) Washington Memo: The newsletter of the Peace Section's Washington Office attempts to inform constituents of matters pending in Congress and under consideration in the Executive branch. Analysis of issues being reviewed by Congress is accompanied with suggestions as to the timing and the appropriate focus for communications which might have a bearing on the actions of government officials.

Sent only to constituents with sufficient interest to request it, the Washington Memo, initially mailed to a Peace Section list of about 200, currently goes to some 1800 church members, peace committees, pastors and church agency staff.

The Hot Line, a supplement to the bi-monthly newsletter, is currently sent to about 700 individuals who wish to be alerted at crucial junctures when their voice would be especially timely in bringing Christian conscience to bear on decisions affecting peace and war, justice and injustice.

Relating to Government

The Peace Section Washington Office functions as an observor post and in an information gathering and dispersing capacity, not as a lobby or advocate of positions to Government. The office does, of course, convey positions to government officials if requested to do so by constituent groups. Its principle function is to facilitate representation to government by the constituents themselves. This is happening in several ways.

1) Delegation of Representatives from Constituent Groups: Inter-Mennonite delegations are from time to time coordinated by the Peace Section staff to come to Washington to represent the concerns of the church. This occurred in 1971 when changes in Conscientious Objector laws were under consideration in Congress, which could have eliminated all church related assignments. Consultation with leading Congressmen of the House and Senate Armed Services Committees and their staff, clearly served to retain church sponsored service opportunities as an option for conscientious objectors.

At the time of the expansion of the bombing in 1972, appointments were also arranged for an inter-Mennonite delegation of eight, to see White House staff and members of the Congress.

2) Calling on Mission and MCC Personnel: Returning personnel from overseas assignments can offer observations of considerable value to government officials who welcome the viewpoints of non-governmental sources. John Wieler (Bangladesh), Atlee Beechey (India), Doug Hostetter (Vietnam), Urbane Peachey (Jordan) and others have shared in a significant way with government leadership. (See addendum for fuller list.) This movement from the servant posture to the prophetic stance would seem to suggest a valid synthesis of our emphasis on "word and deed." An attached addendum also indicates that Mennonite leaders have testified before Congressional committees over a period of 30 years. Our records indicate that the first testimony on issues other than the draft was presented in 1970.

3) The Voice of the People: Perhaps the most significant development of the last several years has been the expanded communication of the man in the pew with representatives in government. Heretofore, the usual approach has been for our denominational bodies to either (1) approve a formal conference statement which was telegrammed or written to the President on behalf of all members or (2) for several denominational

officials and staff to go to Washington for private consultation with one or two government officials. While there will continue to be time when this approach is appropriate, it is essential that the more recent development of equiping local congregations and members to think through the issues and communicate their own convictions be strengthened.

A significant illustration of this occurred when Johannah Gehman returned from Vietnam. The Bally (PA) congregation discussed her experience of working with war orphans. A Washington Memo, calling attention to possible Congressional funding to improve the care of war-orphaned children prompted congregation action to send Johannah, Bo-Cau (her 2 year old adopted Vietnamese orphan) and 4 fellow-members to Washington. The Washington Office arranged their appointments and a powerful witness in sensitizing Congressmen to the suffering of children in war, followed!

While there is the implicit assumption of many that only those in power have the expertise and necessary information to make policy decisions, it can be argued that all sensitive and concerned citizens have a right and responsibility to influence public decisions. The assignment of priorities is not a matter for the expert alone; it does not depend on classified policy decisions which may be ignored if the voice of the church is silent.

HISTORY OF MENNONITE TESTIMONY BEFORE CONGRESS

1940 House Committee on Military Affairs...Amos S. Horst
6/11/45 House Select Committee on Postwar Military Policy... Harold Bender
12/3/45 House Committee on Military Affairs...Harold Bender
4/10/47 President's Advisory Commission on Universal Training... H. S. Bender
3/31/48 Senate Committee on Armed Services...Rev. Don E. Smucker
4/12/48 House Committee on Armed Services...Rev. Albert M. Gaeddert
4/17/48 House Committee on Armed Services...Rev. Albert M. Gaeddert
1/29/51 Senate Preparedness Subcommittee of the Armed Forces Com...H. S. Bender
6/9/55 Senate Committee on Armed Services...Robert Kreider
3/3/59 Senate Committee on Armed Services...Melvin Gingerich
1960 Special Subcommittee on Utilization of Military Manpower of the House Committee on Armed Services... Edgar Metzler
3/12/63 Senate Subcommittee of the Armed Services Com...Alvin J. Beachy
4/14/67 Senate Committee on Armed Services...Dr. Wm. Keeney
5/3/67 House Committee on Armed Services...Bishop John E. Lapp

Non-draft related testimony

8/70 Senate Committee on Finance (written statement by Galen O. Yoder) (Family Assistance Act of 1970)

4/21/71 Senate Subcommittee to Investigate Problems Connected with Refugees and Escapees of the Committee on the Judiciary...Kevin Byrne, written statement by Atlee Beechy with letter from Kurt Sawatsky

6/16/71 Senate Appropriations Subcommittee on Foreign Operations Harry Martens

8/16/72 Senate Subcommittee on Refugees and Escapees...

* * *

MCC and Minorities: Mennonite concern for peace and nonviolence could not avoid glaring social injustices in North American society. During World War II, MCC had a brief concern for the relocation of Japanese Americans. During the 1950's and '60's, voluntary service workers increasingly struggled with the pressure for civil rights by black Americans. Vincent Harding and Titus Bender served as resource persons to churches in the south. The focus of the 1970's has shifted to native Americans in Canada and the United States. Reading 15 reports the crises ministry of Vincent and Rosemarie Harding in Birmingham, Alabama.

Reading 15

MEMORANDUM

TO: Peace Section Executive Committee
FROM: Vincent Harding
SUBJECT: Birmingham, Alabama
DATE: May 30, 1963

Protest demonstrations in Birmingham began on Wednesday, April 3. Though we were out of Atlanta (on a week-long preaching mission at Broad Street Church, Harrisonburg, Virginia) at the time, we had been appraised of their imminence, and had long been pondering our possible role in the situation. On Sunday evening, April 7, we returned to Atlanta in time for Rosemarie to attend a baptismal service at Ebenezer Baptist Church, where Martin King, Jr. serves as co-pastor with his father. Dr. King had come in from Birmingham for the service, and when it was over he called to Rosemarie over the public address system. When she went to him he urged that the two of us come to Birmingham, primarily to try to help establish some creative communications between the Negro and white leaders of the community. (This kind of encounter between Negroes and whites is one of the primary goals of non-violent direct action as Dr. King interprets it).

We remained in Atlanta for the next two days (partly to fulfill commitments there to a National Student Christian Federation group and partly to consider more carefully our calling to Birmingham), and in the course of those days several persons in Atlanta and Birmingham urged us to go to the Alabama city. On Wednesday afternoon, April 10, we drove--with no little fear and trembling--the 165 miles from Atlanta to Birmingham. As is usual in these situations, we were not sure how long we might have to stay. We (Rosemarie, Rachel, and I stayed on the campus of Miles College, a Negro school rather than at the motel which served as headquarters for King and the Birmingham leaders. We wanted to operate as long as possible without being totally identified with them. They understood this. At the outset, however, we needed to spend much of our time simply getting to know some of the local Negro leaders and assessing the direction and depth of the protest movement. (On Good Friday, April 12, we were so caught up in the spirit of the demonstrations that we almost offered ourselves for arrest along with Dr. King.)

Then, we began to make contact with a variety of white persons. In the course of the next week (April 14-20) we were regularly in conference with white clergymen, lawyers, businessmen and political leaders. Initially, our main purpose was fourfold: to give them a chance to talk with Negroes, in mutual confrontation; to interpret the mood and requests of Birmingham's Negroes to them; to understand their point of view; and to bring them in direct face to face contact with local and national Negro leaders. All of these were necessary before fruitful negotiations could begin. With one notable exception (Commissioner Eugene "Bull" Conner) we were able to see all the persons we contacted by phone. Sometimes, the fear of reprisal made it necessary for the meetings to be held in secret places.

By Saturday April 20, it appeared as if the path were open for fruitful conversation between Negroes and whites. Some had already taken place, and more promising ones seemed imminent. Therefore, we felt a little less guilty about leaving Birmingham on Saturday afternoon, April 20, to keep a long standing preaching engagement at Wesleyan University in Middletown, Connecticut, the next day. (The arrival of an experienced mediator, Dr. Allan Knight Chalmeres, the day before we left Birmingham also gave us more courage to leave the situation at that point.)

During those days immediately following, commitments at Akron and Nashville kept us away from Birmingham. Then, news of the impounding of the MCC car by the police sent me back to that city on Thursday morning on April 25. Another commitment in South Georgia took me away the next afternoon, but I had had some opportunity to work briefly at the problem of creative communications before I left. Things were not moving as speedily as we had hoped. (The merchants of the city were rather reticent to move ahead in negotiations without a city government clearly established.) I was ordered to bed by the doctor for a week, April 28-May 5. On Tuesday May 7--the day of the most potentially dangerous demonstration--I returned to Birmingham with Paul Peachey, ostensibly for a four-hour Church Peace Mission planning meeting. However, negotiations began to move with some greater sense of urgency that day and I was asked to stay and take part (first, though, I had to go out on the streets that afternoon and help stop the battle between the fire hoses and the Negro crowd). I remained in the city until Friday, May 10, participating in negotiations, and trying continually to interpret the two groups to each other when negotiations were not in session. On Thursday evening, May 9, Martin King asked me to write the statement that he would release to the press after final agreement had been reached (this should be kept in confidence). The last details of this agreement were ironed out by a small group of us late Thursday and early Friday. Later in the day on May 10, the announcement was made to the press. Unfortunately, I decided to leave Birmingham on that evening and was not there the next night (May 11-12) when the bombs and the crowd exploded. However, I was in constant contact with Negroes and whites by phone, urging a continued commitment to the agreement. By the grace of God, responsible men on both sides kept their heads, and the agreement was not broken.

* * *

The Peace Witness Abroad: During the post World War II epoch, as MCC engaged in relief and reconstruction work in Europe, there was an immediate interest in communicating the Biblical message of peace. North American representatives were influential in organizing an International Mennonite Peace Committee in 1949. Even more significant were the conversations with European Christian spokesmen. Following is a report of the first Puidoux Theological Conference where pacifists and non-pacifists discussed the ethical implications of the Christian gospel. At the same time, the Peace Society was actively urging Mennonite missions in Latin America, Asia, and Africa to make peace and reconciliation central to their message. For full documentation see Donald F. Durnbaugh, Editor, ON EARTH PEACE. Discussions on War/Peace Issues Between Friends, Mennonites, Brethren and European Churches 1935 - 1975. Elgin, Illinois: The Brethren Press, 1978. Pp. 412.

Reading 16

Puidoux Theological Conference, August 15-19, 1955. Report by Albert J. Meyer.

An historic meeting in which a number of theologians

from Lutheran and Reformed churches in Europe met with representatives of the Historic Peace Churches and of the International Fellowship of Reconciliation was held at Cret Bernard, Puidoux (near Lausanne), Switzerland, from August 15 to August 19, 1955. In his introductory remarks, Oberkirchenrat Heinz Kloppenburg of Dortmund, Chairman of the Presiding Committee, emphasized the unusual character of the Conference. It may well have been in the first time in hundreds of years that leaders of the Mennonites and other peace churches grappled with leaders of the Continental state churches in days of discussion on the theological issues that separate them.

From the beginning, the Conference was planned as a meeting of Christian pacifists. Before the growing menace of nuclear war, it is becoming clear both in ecumenical Christianity and in Christian pacifist circles that there is urgent need for a serious re-thinking of the questions of war and peace in relation to the Christian message. Christian pacifists are convinced that non-pacifists have not been true to the way of love implicit in the Gospel. But those holding the position of nonresistance, while agreeing that Christians should not participate in war, have differed widely not only on the Scriptural bases for their peace convictions but also on direct and practical consequences of their beliefs such as whether the Church should ask the State to be nonresistant or not and whether nonresistance should be the expression of the conviction of individuals in the Church or whether the Church should include clear teaching on nonresistance in its discipline. We Mennonites ourselves are not in complete agreement with each other on these questions, and, although we have been increasingly led to express our convictions in mission and relief activities, we have not yet overcome the opinion current in many circles that we are more interested in being pure in isolation from the world than in being obedient in service.

The Puidoux Conference was not held primarily for the purpose of testifying to nonpacifists, then; we realized that as Christians holding the nonresistant position we did not fully understand and agree with each other, and we met to learn in conversation and study of the Word of God together. We did not seek to compromise our individual positions in order to write a common "testimony"; we met in the hope that our willingness to face our differences in an ecumenical spirit and to be guided by the Holy Spirit could itself be a testimony to those who want to discuss intercommunion among Christians without questioning the atomic fratricide that threatens the Church.

The possibility of holding such a conference was first considered at a meeting of the Continuation Committee of the Historic Peace Churches and the International Fellowship of Reconciliation at "Heerewegen," Zeist, Holland, in November 1954. The Continuation Committee had prepared Peace is the Will of God as a testimony to the World Council of Churches before the Evanston Assembly, and discussions that arose in the course of the preparation of this document indicated that further theological conversation among the peace groups, perhaps with the co-operation of theologians from other traditions, was desirable. At a meeting of the Continuation Committee in London in February of this year, John Yoder and Albert Meyer of the Mennonites were asked to prepare a report on issues that should be considered in such a conversation and to present their findings at a meeting of Continuation Committee members with World Council leaders in Geneva in March.

In conversation with Dr. Robert Bilheimer, Director of the Division of Studies, Dr. Elfan Rees of the Churches' Commission on International Affairs, and other World Council leaders, the Continuation Committee learned that everyone was agreed that a pacifist theological conference could provide an important contribution to both pacifist and ecumenical thinking and would not in any way duplicate projects planned by the World Council itself. As the subjects that seemed to demand further study by pacifists were listed, Bilheimer not only gave specific suggestions but also pointed out areas in which pacifist theologians could make useful studies that other ecumenical groups could hardly make at present because of wide varieties of confessional traditions they represent. It was at Geneva that the Continuation Committee asked Brother Heinz Kloppenburg and Albert Meyer to be administrative chairman and administrative secretary, respectively, for the Conference. Professor Hannes de Graaf of the University of Utrecht, Pastor Jean Lasserre of St. Etienne, and Oberkirchenrat Joachim Beckmann of Düsseldorf were asked to serve with Heinz Kloppenburg on the Presiding Committee.

The theme of the Conference was "The Lordship of Christ over Church and State." Papers and discussions were arranged under two sub-topics: (1) "The Relationship of the People of God to the World," and (2) "Is there a Christian Ethic for the State?" Over 110 pages of preliminary theological work papers were printed by the Mennonite Press in Basel and were distributed to participants by the secretariat before the Conference; these included previously unpublished resumes of publications and translations of works by Oscar Cullman, Ernest Wright, Herbert Butterfield, Jean Lasserre, Hannes de Graaf, John W. Miller and John H. Yoder.

After these preparations, the thirty participants from Denmark, England, France, Germany, the Netherlands, Switzerland and the United States net at Puidoux for the four full days of theological discussion. A fuller report on the sessions can be given in an article to follow. Outstanding papers on the "People of God and the World" were given by Ds. Hendrik Bremer (Dutch Mennonite), Professor Ernst Wolf of the University of Göttingen, Dean Harold Bender of Goshen College Biblical Seminary, and Professor H. G. Wood of the Woodbrooke Friends College in England. Dean William Beahm of Bethany Biblical Seminary (Church of the Brethren) and Professor Götz Harbsmeir of the Pädagogisches Institut of Lüneburg contributed to the discussions in an important way. The main studies on the "Christian Ethic for the State" topic were presented by Pastor Jean Lasserre of the French Reformed Church, and by John Yoder of the Mennonites. There were serious and tense discussions--there is no time for levity when men are pleading for a message from the Word of God--but the conversations were in the best brotherly spirit. Several of the German theologians said they were reminded of the atmosphere in the hard days of the Confessing Church, when church leaders were struggling in the face of persecution and possible imprisonment to find the will of God. We felt our need and the need of the world and we truly felt the leading of the Holy Spirit.

We reached some definite conclusions, and yet it was our unanimous conviction that, the Lord willing, discussions of this kind must continue and that we must continue to help each other grow in common confrontations with the Scripture. It was decided that representative members of the Puidoux circle should be responsible for future planning and that the Puidoux study group should henceforth be called "Church and Peace"; Oberkirchenrat Kloppenburg will continue as chairman and the present secretariat arrangement at the Mennonite Central Committee headquarters here in France will be continued.

Several days after Puidoux, I received a communication from Brother Kloppenburg that indicates the spirit in which the "Church and Peace" circle views the future. He wrote: "The Lord be praised!...You cannot overestimate what this encounter means to us Landeskirchen people...I am so happy about these days that the following work can only be still more a matter of prayer than the beginning was."

* * *

Reading 17

Report of November 10, 1960 by Paul Peachey at the conclusion of his service as a peace missioner in Japan and India.

TO: Peace Section Executive Committee
FROM: Paul Peachey
DATE: Nov. 10, 1960
SUBJECT: Reports and Recommendations, East Asia peace witness.

I

Since this will be a critical report, may I preface it with an expression of gratitude to God and to MCC for the privilege to serve in Asia, and of esteem to my Mennonite fellow-workers in Asia, who have demonstrated great dedication and resourcefulness in their labors. I give this expression, not merely because it is due, but also to make certain that I am not misunderstood. For the inadequacies of our effort in Asia are due, not to individual incompetency but to the inadequate idealogized framework within which they labor and of which we are all a part.

Further, the gates of hell shall not prevail against the church in Asia. No one can presume to forsee the counsels of God. As long as it is day, we work. Certainly the work (i.e., churches and evangelistic witness) should be supported and strengthened with all available resources. This report, therefore, does not presuppose that the days of evangelism in Asia are ended. In fact, this report is justified only on the premise that they are not.

II

The march of history has sharply curtailed the growth and spread of Christianity in Asia during the past two decades. Among the many factors occasioning this, the following are outstanding;

1) The total revolution of Asian life now in progress, bringing medicine, education, etc., (whereby missions had initiated their work in Asia) on a comprehensive national scale, has outmoded the mission as the pioneer agency of social change.

2) The revolution in Asia is associated with a spiritual and intellectual renaissance, which means a fresh attempt on the part of millions to discover life's deepest answers in their own cultural and religious heritage.

3) Despite a religious renaissance there is also a profound secularization inspired on the one hand by the faith in human endeavor which accompanied the rise of modern science and technology in the West also, and on the other hand, by the conclusion that all religion is obsolete, having served its role when man was still in a primitive state.

4) In the awakened Asia, missionary endeavor is widely regarded by non-Christians as the religious phase of a now discredited and out-moded imperialism.

These, and other factors, have led to a broad rejection of Christianity as a live or meaningful option for Asia, resulting in attitudes ranging from (often disdainful) indifference (Japan, e.g.) to forthright hostility (China, parts of India, e.g.). The only possible interpretation of events today, humanly speaking, is to conclude that the climax of this reaction still lies in the future.

III

The Western missionary endeavor in Asia was molded by a world order which presupposed: a) an internally static agrarian society in Asia; and b) the domination of Asia and of the world by the technologically and politically stronger West. Operating within this framework virtually all Christian missions were compromised, perhaps willy-nilly, either a) by active participation in political imperial designs (e.g., flagrant examples among both Catholics and Protestants in China) and/or the invocation of imperial power in support of the missionary cause; or b) by passively acquiescing to the attitudes and social relations fostered by the foregoing world order.

Today one finds deep soul-searching in the missionary community, especially among the veterans of work in China. Nevertheless it is doubtful whether anywhere the upheaval in Asia has been adequately faced. In part the upheaval is too vast and profound for human comprehension. But in part also we are limited by the inadequacies of our own Western Christianity; a) the major bodies are still so Constantinian in their ethical outlook that they can neither draw the consequences for Western Christianity nor provide the help they ought to provide the "younger" churches; and b) the newer fundamentalist missions are so engrossed in American individualistic piety, in revivalism and in anti-communism that they can neither criticize themselves nor comprehend what is afoot in Asia. (e.g. the missionary in Japan who, when I raised a few of these matters in explaining my work, beat a quick retreat to higher and safer ground by answering, "I'm glad that all I have to do is to preach the gospel.")

IV

The crisis for America and for American Christians is far more acute than "even Mennonites" assume. This must be recognized, even if the "worst"--nuclear war--can be avoided, which is by no means certain. Two competing and lesser powers today seek to contain or to wield the enormous dynamism of Asia--the one Marxist and "revolutionary", the other capitalist and "counter-revolutionary". It is the bitter irony of history to have cast the United States in a role on the world stage which today must frankly be recognized as counter-revolutionary. As a result our nation has been far more militarized and "fascist-ized" than we imagine, and has allied us with the remnants of decadent and exploitative classes in country after country (Japan, Korea, Taiwan, etc.), and Christianity is used by America as the ideological backbone for a moral-military crusade on a world scale against communism (Cf. S Korean schools and J. Edgar Hoover placard in American schools). Humanly speaking, it is a matter of utter despair as to whether American Christians, much less Americans generally, can ever be brought to face these facts. (That equally sharp or sharper words must be spoken with regard to the communist side goes without saying.)

Not infrequently, therefore, far-seeing Asians and even missionaries have indicated, on learning a bit about our effort, that America and not Asia, is the place where the issue must be attacked. While I would not concur in any suggestion that the task should not be taken up at the Asian end, I do feel profoundly that to carry on in Asia without facing the issue at home more radically than we the Peace Section have is not only futile but, with out our realizing it clearly, perhaps also hypocritical.

Our lag in facing issues at home is reflected then in the orientation and training of the missionaries we American Mennonites send out. Keeping in mind the opening comments of this statement, the remarks in my India report (page 2, #2) and reposing in the confidence of these walls let me say that I did not meet a half dozen Mennonite missionaries in Asia who were at all equipped to wrestle creatively with the issues I here raise. That God nonetheless blesses His work and uses the devoted brethren and sisters we have sent out is no exoneration for our failure at the point which counts (cf. my final report, p. 5, III, #3, where this statement is anticipated.) The inability of these workers as a whole to move imaginatively beyond American Protestantism or fundamentalism and to be open to the new and unusual stirrings of the spirit is simply a reflection of where we stand both here and abroad.

Now admittedly, the Peace Section, which has found itself at times as sort of an uninvited participant, and a short term "outsider" as myself, are hardly in a position to fully assess or to change the situation. Therefore, both in my work and in my interpretation I have always sought to labor as a special minister within the missionary community, recognizing the need for my insights and endeavors to be complemented and judged by the community. But the Peace Section nonetheless must "magnify" its "office" in the Pauline sense. It has been commissioned by the same churches that have commissioned the missions, and has been set up to do a specialized job in a way that the missions have not. The formation of the mission secretaries' committee is therefore only a first step; if in our churches we are called to send workers, by this token we are constrained also to pay the price which this entails.

Against this background I wish to summarize the recommendations I made in my India report (March 30, 1960) and my final Japan-East Asia report (August 10, 1960), with some modifications based on further reflection and consultation with Melvin Gingerich.

A. Our Ongoing Background Work

1) after necessary preparation the Peace Section might approach the mission boards inviting participation in (or to initiate themselves) a thorough, long-range study of the issues raised above, which would entail endeavors such as:

a) continuing working parties, as per: India report recommendation #9: (Everything I saw on this trip would underscore the growing concern for broadening the background training for missionaries. Obviously the missionary task is greater than any possible training in skills...So far as peace and missions are concerned, the most important place to strengthen the witness is in training of out-going missionaries. The Peace Section might well take the matter up with the mission boards and even the colleges. I am not thinking of techniques, of "how to..." courses, but of the deeper questions of the Christian life and its social dimensions.")

Final report recommendations #1

(There must be a constant refinement of objectives and study of issues confronting the total church witness in Asia. Perhaps MCC and the missions together need advisory study groups which will provide background materials for policy people in missions and MCC. A half dozen people in the colleges and elsewhere might have areas of study parcelled out among them concerning which they would confer annually and make reports to the policy people.)

and #3: (I would like to see the Peace Section and the missions look together at the necessity for a somewhat broader mandate than merely "peace" for the program...The concept of the peace worker needs to be studied in the light of broader needs within the missionary effort for specialized work in the field of faith and culture, church and world, in the (pagan) environment in which the new churches are being established. Closely akin to this is the need for specialized theological leadership among the missionaries themselves as they wrestle with the complex tasks of church building. Many would more readily comprehend the importance of church building. Many would more readily comprehend the importance of the peace effort if it were couched in broader terms as these.)

b) Perhaps a major inter-Mennonite conference (board representatives, missionaries, etc.)

c) Facing the ecumenical question

India report recommendation #10: (The Mennonite churches in India will be confronted increasingly with the ecumenical question, and any conversation with Christians outside our immediate circle becomes at once an ecumenical (no necessary connection with Geneva) conversation. Certainly one cannot counsel the world to accept Christ and to find reconciliation rather than fighting it out, without also taking seriously the denominational or other estrangement from the brother next door....There are now in India several movements for church union, movements which so far unfortunately have consisted of conversations or mergers on the level of denominational structures. The question still to be faced by the Mennonite churches and missions is that of their relationship to each other, to the larger Christian community in India and to Christians abroad. Without room for fuller discussion, I shall not hazard a recommendation...

Final report #7

(In developing a policy for the entire area at some point fresh consideration must be given to our relations to a) other Christian peace efforts as FOR (should our worker, e.g., belong) and b) WCC, WEF, etc. This coming summer the WEF is planning both regional and world meetings in Asia and next year the WCC meets in Delhi. It is my own conviction, a conviction somewhat tested by the experience of these three years, that at least in Asia we must seek deep relations in both groups (WCC and WEF) and their respective constituencies. Probably the mission secretaries' committee should take the matter up in a previously informed discussion, recognizing that they cannot presume thereby to make the decisons that the Christians in Asia must make for themselves.)

d) Better preparation for missionaries (India, #9, previous page.

2) The Peace Section will need to take seriously the training of some workers on its own, looking especially to veterans of MCC work in Asia, missionaries.

3) The Peace Section will need to take up at a serious level the broader implications of nonresistance (economic, taxes, relation to distribution of surplus foods, foreign aid, etc.) in the light of the counter-revolutionary character of US policy and outlook.

4) Recognizing that with the exception of the actual refusal to bear arms, American Mennonites are often a mission field, rather than an evangelistic remnant, for peace, we (Peace Section) need to examine earnestly the spiritual mandate under which the section works.

B. <u>Program: At Home</u>

1) Presupposing A., we ought to examine earnestly at an

early date our peace witness within American Christianity (including Mennonites, particularly also in the light of Peace Section experience in Europe, in CPM and in Asia, with a view to initiating corresponding steps in America.

2) We need to prepare, in consultation with the various Mennonite missions, a series of non-sectarian Anabaptist materials, speaking to the modern world, with minimal historical reference, in a form suitable for use by missions or churches in non-Western countries, either in English or by translation.

1) The sending of a worker with adequate theological, philosophical, historical and Oriental training to India as per India recommendation #11, and final report recommendation #2, with part India, part East Asia assignment, holds top priority.

India: (Edward Benedict has recommended the establishment of a peace center (literature, study groups, etc.) in Calcutta. (Douglas Steere, of the Philadelphia Quakers, in India recently, urged that either jointly or singly the HPC open such centers in the major cities of India. The Quakers have a center already in New Delhi, the Brethren might logically open one in Bombay and we in Calcutta). He also recommends the location of the East Asia Peace Section representative in Calcutta. Further, he recommends the use of some PAX men in a Ford Foundaton program. In principle I would fully endorse these proposals, except that not having toured the whole area in question, I am not fully certain as yet as to the best location for an East Asia office. Also, before selecting Calcutta as a base we would need to explore questions such as the relationship to EFI see above #4), the NCC. etc. In practice, India needs its own full time worker, in addition to the East Asia coordinator, who may or may not find Calcutta the feasible base.)

Final: (Now that a worker has been assigned to Japan at the earliest possible date someone needs to be sent with broader East Asia responsibilities. For the immediate future such a worker might well be based in Calcutta, giving a major portion of his time to India. The purpose would be to develop the effort within India similarly to what we have done in Japan while at the same time steps would be taken to tie things together internationally.)

As to the immediate tasks in India cf. India report recommendations 1, 2, 3, 4, 7, 8 (not reproduced here) and on Asia, see final recommendation #7 as listed above, p. 5, top.

Note also necessity of prior clearance with the missions.

2) Equally urgent in my mind is the need to pursue with the Relief Section, on the one hand, and with the Mennonite mission boards on the other, the need for what I shall call a new "missionary-service presence in Asia, notably India, as per India report recommendations #5 and 6: (In view of

the need to a) meet the Gandhians, Bhoodan, etc. at a deeper level, and b) to relate ourselves more fruitfully to the Indian revolution, I would like to see some young agriculture or science college graduates go into the Gandhian village schemes. This they (the Gandhians) would welcome warmly. It would require a more mature person than we usually send out under PAX...the Indian FOR should be asked to help in advisory capacity, to mediate between us and the Gandhians, which they would be happy to do.

Similarly, men of the same caliber might well be sent into the Mennonite missions, to work out from the missions into government village schemes in informal advisory capacity. Most Mennonite missions do some informal extension work which could be enhanced by such assistance....The most frequent answer to the question: can we still help? (after all the reaction against missions, imperialism, etc.): Send us people (not money), simply to live among us and show us how.

Cf. also my Aug. 10, 1960 memo to Wm. Snyder

3) The frequently mentioned question of inter-Mennonite relations in Asia needs study, particularly in the light of steps already taken (Bender-Graber correspondence, early 1960).

4) In the ongoing Peace Section relationship to Japan, in which so far as the total witness is concerned (as distinct from the administration) remains in the Peace Section picture, two items require further study: 1) How far shall we pursue the historical study of Christianity and peace in Japan? and 2) How far is it appropriate for the Peace Section to work at the still unresolved questions of American-Japanese Christian relations regarding the past war and the present rearmament of Japan?

Final report recommendations 6, 5

(The advisory committee has approved a proposal that we carry on some historical study on Christianity and peace in Japan as part of the ongoing program there, to provide the necessary background for our effort. I began to collect a few materials in Tokyo and have checked further with the Missionary Research Library in New York. While for the moment it is not a matter of ...publication, though I hope to publish a preliminary survey, perhaps in MQR, a missionary to Japan might pick the matter up at a later date as a graduate thesis... Thinking in long range terms we must develop as clear a grasp as possible of the course of Christianity in Asia, during the Protestant era particularly, as it relates to revolution, nationalism, imperialism and war. (Since conversations between American and Japanese Christians on the whole range of contemporary and postwar political problems deeply affecting church life on both sides, though less consciously so in former, has been inadequate and unhealthy, the Peace Section should prepare a careful approach whereby the Mennonite missions at both ends (US and Japan) would seek to initiate...some conversations aimed at strengthening and deepening the ties and understanding between the churches of the two countries, and to clarify the present cloudy atmosphere surrounding questions of Christian involvement in the past war and the present military pacts...)

D. A final comment regarding objectives. The new statement drawn up after Wm. Snyder's tour to Asia is adequate for the present, as I understand our needs, and I see no need for revision at present. Its translation into program is something else, of course. Melvin Gingerich stresses, and I concur, that in any case we need to help Asian Christians to understand that there have after all been Christians in the West who did not accept militarism and its attendant evils; further, that we need to confront people with these demands. He stresses likewise the importance of sending a worker who has a mature awareness (rather than something recently acquired) of the depth of the Asia revolution.

PS. In looking at these long and cumbersome suggestions, I recognize that they cannot all be undertaken simultaneously and perhaps some of them never. I have tried to limit myself nonetheless to the type of proposals that I do consider realistic in terms of our policy, experience and resources.

* * *

Capital Punishment: Among the many aspects of witness to peace has also been MCC concern for offender ministries and representation to government on capital punishment. The following July, 1978 statement makes reference to two cases in which hatred was met with love, and proposes that Mennonites might constitute redemptive communities in which criminals could find healing and faith.

Reading 18

Summary Statement on H. R. 13360, Death Penalty Proceedings, by Delton Franz, Washington Office, MCC:

(1) Several brief "case studies" of capital crimes involving individuals and the Mennonite church community are cited in our full statement illustrating the historic position of the Mennonite churches (an historic peace church) both in respect to our opposition to capital punishment by the State and our response to defendants who have taken the life of another (including members of our church).

(2) With respect to the post-conviction proceedings outlined in H.R. 13360, the "mitigating" and "aggravating" circumstances provide, we believe, more helpful criteria

than has been available to date for assessing the culpability of the convicted defendant. If there must be a death penalty - and we are opposed to the same - these guidelines bring our criminal justice system a step beyond the inequitable judicial process our society has known in the past.

(3) However, we do not believe that either counsel or the jury can sufficiently uncover or comprehend the complex, interlocking "mitigating" and "aggravating" circumstances to possess the necessary wisdom to impose a sentence of death. For that reason, from both a sociological perspective and on theological grounds, the mitigating circumstances must always outweigh the aggravating circumstances. Man's Creator alone is wise enough to pass judgment on a life.

(4) We ask whether the "mitigating" circumstances would allow for and include the responsiveness of a redemptive community taking the initiative to receive and offer support for the convicted defendant. The church has much to offer the criminal justice system in this area. And does the bill before the committee allow for a repentant defendant?

Statement on the Death Penalty
by
Delton Franz, Director,
Washington Office of Mennonite Central Committee
for
Ohio and Eastern Conference (The Mennonite Church)
Central District Conference (General Conference Mennonite)
Mennonite Central Committee, Peace Section
Presented at Hearings of the Committee on the Judiciary
July 19, 1978

As representatives of the Mennonite church, we appreciate the opportunity to present this statement for the House Judiciary Committee's considerations, as you weigh the direction that legislation should take regarding this nation's use of the death penalty within the criminal justice system.

While we do not pretend to speak for all Mennonites, the observations and experiences shared here do, we believe, reflect the current and historic convictions of a large proportion of our membership.

From the sixteenth century to the present, many Mennonites have witnessed against capital punishment. One of the charges against Felix Manz, the first Anabaptist (Mennonite) martyr, was that he had rejected capital punishment.

In 1910 Daniel Kauffman, Mennonite leaders, said: "The taking of human life, whether upon the field of battle, on the gallows or in the electric chair, or in a conflict between individuals, belongs to uncivilized nations." C. Henry Smith, Mennonite historian, said in 1932: "Human life to the Mennonites is sacred, and not to be snuffed out for any reason whatsoever, individually or collectively, . . . to appease the demand for public justice . . ."

We turn now to an overview of our nation's entrapment in violence, in the hope that her people might heed the words of the prophet: "As I live, says the Lord, I take pleasure not in the death of the wicked, but in the turning back of the wicked who change their ways to win life." (Ezekiel 33:11)

Our Nations's Proclivity for Violence

More than seventy nations have acted to reduce human violence by abolishing the death penalty. Among advanced nations, the United States remains the chief advocate of death as a punishment for crime. We are characterized in the eyes of millions as much by our executions as by the general violence of our heavily armed population. Indeed the two phenomena blur into one.

Our emotions may cry for vengeance in the wake of a horrible crime, but we know that killing the criminal cannot undo the crime, will not prevent similar crimes by others, does not benefit the victim, destroys human life and brutalizes society. If we are to still violence, we must cherish life. Executions cheapen life.

A humane and generous concern for every individual, for his safety, health and fulfillment, will do more to soothe the savage heart than the fear of state-inflicted death. So long as government takes the life of its citizens, the sixth commandment from the Law of Moses, "Thou shalt not kill", the foundation of Judaic law and Christian ethics, will lose influence we have claimed Mosaic law has had upon our own legal system. The spiral of violence and retribution must be halted. George Bernard Shaw said: "Murder and capital punishment are not opposites that cancel one another, but similars that breed their kind."

Our society imprisons the ghetto teenager who pulls a gun on the corner grocer, awards medals to soldiers who kill sons of the enemy in war, and posthumously honors generals who give orders to pilots to incinerate thousands of innocent civilians with bombs from 20,000 feet altitude. The blame diminishes as the violence increases. Can a society that teaches its sons that mass killings in war are honorable while the single face-to-face act is criminal, expect to cultivate a true reverence for life?

The time is long overdue in our country to begin the process of reversing violence by eliminating it within our criminal justice system. We can begin by curbing the proliferation of weapons through over-the-counter sales, establishing alternatives to our archaic prison system - a system that exacerbates the crime problem - and finally by eradicating that most futile of all responses to crime . . . the gas chambers, the electric chairs, the gallows, and the firing squads.

In our judgment, the only meaningful response to capital crimes is to work for the removal and alleviation of the causes of violence. And while violence will never be eradicated, the State's response with still further violence (capital punishment) is neither morally defensible nor proven to be scientifically or sociologically effective as a deterrent.

We do not mean to suggest that any neat or simple answers to violence are available from the religious community. Often to the shame of the churches, we have tolerated violence and indeed perpetrated it by our silence and consent to the actions of the State in the taking of life. It is, therefore, important that from our religious traditions we lift up for ourselves, our children and our government - those unheralded but significant and courageous witnesses that have been made to honor the sanctity of life. Only when more of us are inspired to perserving life, can the frightening spiral of death be abated.

BRIEF CASE STUDIES IN ALTERNATIVES TO VIOLENCE AND CAPITAL PUNISHMENT

A Youth Worker's Death in the Ghetto

Our conscience on violence and retribution continues to find expression in the younger generation. The real guidelines for how public officials, private individuals and the Christian community respond to violent acts must emerge from deep moral principles grounded in real life situations.

On October 2, 1973, Evelyn Wagler, a 24-year-old, German-born Swiss immigrant was set upon by several teenage youth in a ghetto of Boston, where she had moved only a week earlier. Carrying a can of gasoline to start her stalled car, she was accosted by the youths who dragged her into an alley, forced her to pour the gasoline over her body, threw a match and she turned into a human torch.

After taping her last words, before her death in Boston City Hospital five hours later, the police called her husband Mark, a Mennonite whom she first met in her native Switzerland, informing him and their four-year-old Jorg Thoreau (names after an early 16th century Anabaptist Mennonite leader and the American writer and naturalist) that their wife and mother had been murdered.

The police at her bedside, attempted through a taped interview to obtain some evidence that would enable them to apprehend the youth. Evelyn's last request was, nevertheless, that retribution not be made against the youth.

Evelyn and Mark had experienced a real and sobering exposure to the poverty, desperation and injustices experienced by blacks in the ghetto during their participation in a Mennonite youth service project on Chicago's south side. They understood why black youth would tell whites "to get out of our neighborhood" as Evelyn's assailants had on the night of her death. It is not unreasonable to believe that Evelyn became a surrogate victim in Boston's Roxbury area, for the oppressors the ghetto victims were really trying to get at, "Mr. Charlie".

An article in the November 11, 1973 New York Times Magazine, indicated that investigative officers, based on a rash of equally barbarous crimes in Boston within a three-day period, linked the manner in which Evelyn was killed to the film "Fuzz". It was shown on ABC TV in Boston just two days before her death, protraying delinquent youth on the Boston waterfront dousing tramps with gasoline and setting them on fire.

Commenting on the loss of his wife, Mark said, "She had been killed by the system that creates ghettos and racial hatred. That's the way Evelyn would have looked at it too. The last thing she would have wanted was for her death to be used to incite people" (to retribution). In life and even in death, Evelyn and Mark sought to break the cycle of violence. Mark said the one thought that kept recurring in his mind and freed him from a spirit of retribution was a Biblical passage: "Vengeance is mine, I will repay, says the Lord."

Application to H.R. 13360

Not suprisingly, this is the kind of capital crime that inevitably arouses the public's cry for the death penalty. I can understand this response. Evelyn and her husband Mark were married in the inner city congregation I pastored and they had a leading role in our community youth programs.

Boston mayor Kevin White, in a press conference following Evelyn's death, said: "This is one of the most horrible crimes in our history." For quite obvious reasons the national news media cited the crime as a heinous act. This incident would appear to explicitly portray aggravating circumstance #2 in H.R. 13360: "Wanton and intentional cruelty or depravity was shown in the course of the offense."

Yet under H.R. 13360, "Mitigating Circumstances" #1 - ("youthfulness of the defendant(s)") and #2 ("the defendant's capacity to appreciate the wrongfulness of the . . . conduct . . .") might have a bearing as well.

While the aggravating circumstances are very compelling in the Wagler death, an eleven-year involvement in an impoverished, densely populated inner city ghetto also compells one to weigh heavily the impact of "mitigating circumstances" on those who took Evelyn's life. Consequently, I must ask:

Can a jury be expected to adequately perceive and weigh the many mitigating factors relevant to such a tragedy? How might high unemployment, inferior educational opportunity, and over-crowded slum housing have contributed to the lack of a positive self-image, the reinforcement of failure and eventually violent, anti-social behavior? Numerous scientific and psychological studies have been done to examine the relationship of these conditions to crimes of violence.

A common, momentary escape for those living in such conditions has been television. What then is the impact of television violence on youth and adult defendants convicted of violent crimes? After hundreds of formal scientific studies and decades of contentious debate, reasonable people are obliged to agree that televised violence does indeed have harmful effects on human character and attitudes.

The U.S. Surgeon General, as long ago as 1972, said after delivering to Congress one of the most exhaustive ($1 million, three-year) research projects ever undertaken by social scientists:

"There comes a time when the data are sufficient to justify action. The overwhelming consensus (is) that televised violence does have an adverse affect on certain members of society."

In the six years since that declaration by the Surgeon General, TV watchers have been treated to uncounted thousands of brutal homicides, rapes, robberies, muggings, and all-out mayhem. One scientist estimates that by the age of 15, the average child will have witnessed 13,400 televised killings. In 1973, 74, violence occurred in 73 percent of all TV programs, according to the Violence Profile published by the Annenberg School of Communications at the University of Pennsylvania.

Can juries adequately take into account the extent to which the pervasive influence of TV violence has become a significant influence in a defendant's crime of violence, and thereby adequately decide for or against the death penalty?

Response of Amish Community Breaks Spiral of Violence

In 1957, a 19-year-old youth shot and fatally wounded Paul Coblentz, a young Holmes County Ohio farmer. Coblentz was an Old Order Amish Mennonite whose death stirred Holmes County, one of the major centers of Amish population in the country, in an unusual way. Their reaction to the brutal act of this intruder from outside their community surprised the people of eastern Ohio.

Over twenty Amish residents of Holmes County were summoned for jury duty, but all were dismissed as possible jurors because of their unwillingness to inflict the death penalty. As the trial proceeded, many Amish families invited the parents of the slayer into their homes. After the death penalty was handed down by the jury, large numbers of Amish families signed petitions and wrote the Governor of Ohio, requesting a commutation of the sentence. Seven hours before the scheduled execution of Cleo Peters, the Governor granted commutation.

Two ministers visited Peters in the Ohio penitentiary shortly after, learning that Peters had become a Christian several months earlier, deeply appreciative of the letters he had received from Amish people, among them the widow of his victim.

Application to H.R. 13360

It is generally assumed that the public response to the perpetrator of a capital crime will be a cry for his or her execution. But there are numerous instances in which the family and friends of the victim have asked that revenge not be taken and that help be sought to rehabilitate the defendant. Such was the response of the Coblentz family, their fellow church and community members. Their redemptive attitude had a positive impact on the defendant resulting ultimately in the commutation of his execution.

Question: Should not such ameliorative responses to a violent crime be considered a mitigating circumstance? Does not the attitude of those in the community from which a defendant comes and to which, if rehabilitated, he/she may hopefully return, have a bearing on jury deliberations? This question must be addressed to all of us who are affiliated with the church, as well as to you the members of Congress, but we believe the untapped community resources for a redemptive rather than simply a retributive response are present in our society. These people-resources could be utilized to a much greater degree.

Furthermore, would the jury's weighing of aggravating and mitigating circumstances as outlined in the procedures of H.R. 13360 allow for the possibility of repentance - turning in a new direction - by the defendant? While a repentant defendant and a redemptive community may sound like irrelevant theological rhetoric, we would suggest that these terms can be much more than theological abstractions. Criminals often do change from violent to constructive human beings when acceptance and understanding are offered. Perhaps these contingencies do not conform with the procedures outlined in the present legislation before this committee, but we are convinced that the potential of the redemptive community in relating to the potentially repentant defendant is a profound dimension that should not be overlooked by our criminal justice system.

Conclusion: God, Not Man, Final Judge

The procedures in H.R. 13360, while in many respects an improvement over the more arbitrary course followed presently in our judicial proceedings, cannot, in our opinion adequately alleviate the prejudicial influences within our society, affecting prosecutors, jurors and trial judges - in short, all those involved in the criminal justice system. We are further concerned that the 'preponderance of the evidence" submitted by counsel for the defense - as required to establish the mitigating circumstances - can, at best, be limited to the evidence readily accessible. We believe that the evidence available would in many cases be far too limited to adequately inform the jury to make a judgment so final, so all encompassing as the sentence of death.

If indeed, counsel for the defense could adequately know, understand and present to the jury all of the factors contributing to the defendant's crime, - and the jury could, in turn, truly weigh the relationship of these mitigating circumstances to the aggravating circumstances - we might concede that theoretically the jury would then be sufficiently knowledgeable and wise to sit in judgment over the life of the defendant. However, such wise and perfect judgment has not, we believe, been given to the created human order, but continues to remain within the province of the Creator, who alone can be the perfect giver and taker of life.

The critical question is how we - the church and the state - can best foster respect for life and preserve the dignity of the human person. We do not believe that more deaths are the answer. We therefore have to seek methods of dealing with violent crime that will protect society without destroying the offender. In the sight of God, correction of the offender has to take preference over punishment, for it is God's will that humanity be saved, not condemned.

The final arbiter and judge over the "Cains" who have been slain by their brothers "Abel" will be God the Creator, not man . . . not government. While government must maintain an ordered and just society - bringing offenders to a fair trial - these cases, we believe, cannot morally be consumated with the killing of the offender.

When Cain had slain his brother Abel, the Lord put a mark on Cain, "lest any who came upon him should kill him."

In the ancient Biblical understanding of civilized social order - "cities of refuge" were established to which those guilty of violence could retreat until the passion of revenge by their neighbors had subsided. These "cities of refuge" marked significant progress from primitivism toward civilization. Our society by sanctioning the killing of offenders, would take a step backward toward primitivism.

2. Mennonite Mental Health Services (MMHS)

The involvement of MCC in mental health work underlines once again the profound influence which the CPS experience had upon MCC program/planning. The interest and concern of CPS men who had served in mental hospitals fostered a growing conviction that the churches should be involved in mental health work. The first proposal that Mennonites establish a program of care for the mentally ill was made in 1944.

Reading 19

Annual Meeting Minutes, December 28-29, 1944. Minute 26.

"Henry A. Fast spoke briefly concerning the need for a program of care for Mennonites who are mentally ill and proposed serious consideration of the desirability of establishing such a program in a central institution under the administration of the Mennonite Central Committee. Moved and passed to refer this matter to the MCC constituent groups for whatever expression they may have to give."

Reading 20

Executive Committee Meeting Minutes, June 9, 1945. Minute 26.

Moved and passed that we note this action and in the light of our annual meeting action a special Mental Hospital Study Committee be appointed to make preliminary studies in regard to this matter and report to the Executive Committee after the return of H. A. Fast and O. O. Miller from their foreign service--this committee to be composed of P. C. Hiebert, H. S. Bender, and Robert Kreider."

* * *

Within six months this committee had prepared its initial report.

Reading 21

Excerpts, Report of the Mental Hospital Study Committee to the Annual Meeting, December 28-29, 1945.

The Civilian Public Service program has awakened our Church to a whole area of need which we have somewhat neglected--the care of the mentally ill. Approximately 1500 young men and women will have served in the 29 mental hospital and training school units administered by the MCC.

We recognize that the Christian has a responsibility to the mentally ill and the mentally deficient. Christ came teaching, preaching and healing. His was a ministry of healing. As followers of our Master, we are constrained to bring to our fellowmen the ministry of healing. Our responsibility extends not only to those who suffer physical illness but to those who are ill in mind and soul. Paul, the Apostle, called his followers to this responsibility: "Now we exhort you, brethren, warn them that are unruly, comfort the feebleminded, support the weak, be patient toward all men." . . .

This is background to the data compiled from questionnaires sent to the ministers of 1070 Mennonite and Brethren in Christ congregations. We received a 62 percent response with 670 replies. These 670 ministers report of their church communities the following: 302 mentally ill in institutions; 365 mentally ill cared for at home; 68 mentally deficient in institutions; and 500 mentally deficient cared for at home. This is a reported 1235 mentally ill and mentally deficient for 670 congregations. We estimate that information from the remaining 400 congregations would not increase our total more than twenty percent.

In the questionnaire sent to Mennonite ministers was this question: "Do you think the church should establish institutions for our mentally ill and our feeble minded?" Mennonite ministers registered their overwhelming approval of such program. Of 670 replies, 317 approved the proposed program. An additional 111 gave qualified approval. Opposition was voiced by 67.

Letters were sent to fourteen non-Mennonite psychiatrists and mental hospital administrators for their opinions on Mennonite-operated mental institutions or psychiatric departments in general hospitals. Professional opinion is weighted on the side of psychiatric department approach. Two felt that mental hospital administration was not a function of the church. Interviews with three additional mental hospital superintendents indicate added support to the proposal that the church start with psychiatric departments in conjunction with present general hospitals.

Recommendations

On the basis of our studies and our present knowledge of the subject, we have several tentative recommendations to make. These are primarily suggestions for further consideration:

1. This is an interim report of the Mental Hospital Study Committee. There is much valuable information on the subject which must be assembled before any final decisions are made. We recommend that this report be circulated among

church leaders and an effort made to secure their studied judgment based on this information. We propose to present to the MCC a final and complete report by April 1, 1945.

2. Mennonites in the United States own and operate nine general hospitals. We would encourage several of these hospitals to give serious consideration to the establishment of psychiatric wards in conjunction with their hospital program.

3. We would encourage conference groups or regional groups to consider carefully the wisdom of establishing convalescent homes or farms for the care of the chronically mentally ill and other homes for the care of the mentally deficient.

4. We recommend that the MCC continue its program of volunteer service units in state mental institutions. These units serve two major purposes: They are channels for significant public service and they are valuable educational experiences for the young people of the church--"training in service."

5. We are not convinced that the conference groups should at this time share in the establishment of a separate institution for the care of the mentally ill. Major considerations are: Expense, difficulty of securing a convenient geographical location, and the dearth of professional psychiatric personnel. As the necessary resources become available, the conviction may later emerge that we together are prepared to establish a church mental institution and perhaps also a home for the feeble minded.

6. Our major recommendation is that young Mennonite doctors and pre-medics be encouraged to specialize in the field of psychiatry. We trust that talented young men will be led to serve in this neglected area of Christian service.

Submitted by
MENTAL HOSPITAL STUDY COMMITTEE
P. C. Hiebert
Harold Bender
Robert Kreider

* * *

The first concrete development came in 1946.

Reading 22

Executive Committee Meeting Minutes, September 14, 1946.

SEPTEMBER 14, 1946, EXECUTIVE COMMITTEE, MINUTES

19. O. O. Miller proposed the use of the Leitersburg (Hagerstown) MCC farm for a rest home for Mennonites needing

mental care (mild cases) inasmuch as the CPS unit there is closed now.

20. Moved and passed to authorize holding the Leitersburg farm and continuing farm operations after the CPS unit is closed, and request the Executive Secretary to bring to the next meeting a plan which might be considered for the operations of a rest home for mental patients at this place.

Reading 23

Excerpts, Considerations and Recommendations on possibility of utilizing Leitersburg, Maryland farm as Mental Rest Home, Presented to Special Called Meeting of the MCC conjoint with the MCC Aid Section, October 31, 1946.

II. Recommendations to Mennonite Central Committee

A. Recommend using the MCC owned farm at Leitersburg, Maryland as rest home for mentally ill, primarily for Mennonite and Brethren in Christ constituency to be administered by the Mennonite Central Committee.

B. Recommend appointment of a committee of three to serve one year term to recommend to MCC Executive Committee basic policies for such an institution and to be available for advisory purposes.

C. The following recommendations on policy are given as initial suggestions subject to modification by the Executive Committee as necessary.

1. Types of patients to be served: Broadly speaking there are two groups of mental illnesses. They are: (a) Chronic mental illnesses where deterioration and senility make recovery impossible thus making permanent hospitalization necessary. (b) Acute mental illnesses of shorter duration where physical and mental deterioration has not done irreparable damage and where the prognosis is hopeful.

Of the first group we would want a limited number in our home. Our greatest contribution to them is custodial care in a home environment with understanding and loving care. In this group there will be a limited turnover and a minimum of treatment. Their contribution to the farm and house work will be somewhat limited due to their infirmity and their inability to follow instructions.

Of the second group we would want a proportionate number and it is in respect to these that our institution would be experimental. It would be our plan to bring patients into a homelike atmosphere maintaining the highest Christian standards of care to administer at a relatively low cost a type of treatment that is almost universally recognized as highly effective.

We would naturally limit ourselves to those patients who are of a non-violent nature who would not endanger self or others. Although the violent patient often has the best prognosis it is conceivable that the care of such patients is more costly and he is often legally involved thus complicating his status.

The second group of patients often go to a state mental hospital and because of inadequate facilities or limited help he is not given the treatment his case requires. In other instances treatment is given but when a patient comes back on the regular wards the abuse and incompetency of the ward attendants undo all the good that had been accomplished.

With the administering of electric shock, which is now the standard treatment for many mental illnesses, and high Christian standards it is to be expected that marvels could be accomplished. Electric shock could be given by an interested doctor in the community who could serve on a consultative basis. The psychiatrist service would be held at a minimum but some arrangement to make one available when needed is indispensable for this type of patient.

It may also be advisable and possible to arrange with state institutions to accept from them such patients from our own conference constituencies as have finished a course of treatment and are recovering. The environment in our institution would conceivably be very conducive to a more rapid recovery.

It is at this point where our rest home would have its "growing edge" and be experimental not only for our own constituency but for all society. We would want to find the right combination of Christian care, home like atmosphere, high personnel standards, reasonable financial policies, and the optimum of scientific therapies of demonstrated value.

2. Application and admission

The home will be primarily for mentally ill from MCC constituency. To determine which applicants are to be admitted the procedure should provide for use of an application form and report from a medical doctor. Before any patient is finally admitted he would be given a psychiatric examination. It is assumed that only voluntarily committed patients will be accepted. Tentative plans would provide for accomodation of at least twenty patient. . . .

III. In Conclusion

It is our conviction that the nature, location, and availability of the farm, need for better care of our own mentally ill, the interest and experience gained by our constituent group through Civilian Public Service and the desire to express the compassionate love of God for the sick of mind--all contribute to the leading of the Lord and point toward this present open door of service. To do more than a custodial job for a limited type of mental illness requires, it would seem, our joint efforts as Mennonite and Brethren in Christ groups. After the home has found its scope of service, and our churches have gained more experience in this field, it may be that individual conferences will establish at such a time similar homes elsewhere. It may even be desirable for an individual conference to assume responsibility for this proposed mental rest home.

October 17, 1946
Elmer M. Ediger

* * *

At its Annual Meeting in January, 1947, MCC decided definitively to begin an active mental health program.

Reading 24

Homes for Mentally Ill Additional Planning, Presented to Executive Committee Meeting, May 2, 1947.

Referring to the following minute 26 of the recent January 3, 1947 annual meeting:

"WHEREAS the Civilian Public Service program--in which approximately 1500 young men and women have served in the 29 mental hospital and training school units administered by the MCC--has awakened our church to a whole area of need which we have somewhat neglected, and

"WHEREAS from this same group and others there is evidence of growing conviction that our church should promptly enter into this service, and

"WHEREAS the special Mental Hospital Study Committee's report, as well as other similar studies in the United States, indicates the extent of this need among us, as well as in the country at large and the generally inadequate facilities for meeting it, and

"WHEREAS none of our individual groups has had experience in serving in this area of need, even though all of our groups have expressed deep concern concerning it, and

"WHEREAS a number of requests have come to us from constituent groups and individuals that through the Mennonite Central Committee such service be initially undertaken as representative of the concern of us all and for initial experience for us all, it is hereby recommended:

(1) that the Mennonite Central Committee propose to make its offices and facilities available for leading out in the initiation of this service.

(2) that an advisory and planning committee of seven members be appointed to proceed immediately with the further study of ways and means and planning along the foregoing lines and to make their recommendations to the Executive Committee

or special sessions of the MCC for further implementation.

(3) that plans be made for three small homes for mentally ill and/or rest homes--one each to be located in the eastern, middle west, and western parts of the United States.

(4) that the Leitersburg, Maryland, CPS farm project be held available for the purposes of this work in the East.

(5) that until the plans are developed further and a special budget presented for action by the Committee as a whole, the costs of the further study and planning be charged to CPS funds,"

the Executive Committee immediately following appointed a Homes for Mentally Ill Planning and Advisory Committee, /This name was changed to Mental Health Service Committee in 1949. The committee was advisory to MCC, not a decision-making body, although MCC rarely rejected or modified recommendations submitted by the committee./ Members: Henry A. Fast, Chairman, Titus Books, Dr. Paul Nase, Henry R. Martens, Harold Sherk, E. C. Bender, Orie O. Miller. This committee as a whole met twice since, January 25 and April 19, and a sub-committee from it with representation from the Akron office met with a representative group from the west coast constituency at Reedley, California, on March 25.

* * *

Plans for creating a mental health facility at Leitersburg were implemented rapidly and in January, 1949, the first patients were admitted to the center, which had been renamed Brook Lane Farm.

Plans for the other two proposed homes--on the west coast and in the middle west--also received immediate attention, but these programs developed more slowly. Reading 25 illustrates some of the options considered by one regional committee, and Reading 26 outlines the program's achievements by 1950.

Reading 25

Review of Considerations to date for Mennonite Mental Health Service in Kansas - Central U.S. Area, June 1, 1948.

There are various factors that have led us as a church to become interested in serving the mentally ill. There is need for additional good care and treatment facilities for mentally ill. We believe Christians should be able to render a unique service because of the value of love in dealing with those in fear, despair, etc., and because basically and potentially Christian faith should be able to help individuals to become "whole" again. Our CPS experiences particularly demonstrated the need for additional good facilities and the value of the way of love. Our concern begins with our own church family but includes more. We are further motivated because this may well be a good channel of our rendering a constructive public service during peace as well as war time, which at the same time gives unique opportunity to witness to the way of peace and love. We believe our church group is uniquely called to explore further this opportunity of service as Christians.

Early in the discussions of Brook Lane Farm, Hagerstown, Maryland, the following possibilities already challenged us: (1) to provide a Christian environment, (2) to retain as much of the homelike framework as possible, (3) to utilize the rural environment where the mentally ill can be closer to God's creative and recreative powers, and (4) to provide personalized care at more economical rates than usually available in private institutions.

Dr. Felix of the U.S. Public Health Service, Mental Hygiene Division, encouraged us very much to go ahead in this field. He gave particular encouragement that at one location we have a more complete service. He suggested a psychopathic hospital for treatment cases only, where special psychiatric training could also be provided, where a psychologist could assist in counseling outpatients. He suggested another home could serve the chronic cases.

The Gheel, Belgium, plan has also been a challenging concept in that a relatively small central institution could be serving a much larger number who would be absorbed in various community homes in a wholesome way.

The nature of the Kansas MCC constituency community in compact geographical area and the presence of three constituent colleges, three general hospitals, various homes for aged has always suggested itself as the logical place for such a more complete Mennonite Mental Health service including some special training facilities.

The Brook Lane Farm hospital project began with the "in-between" concept--that of serving patients between the treatment at the hospital and the home to which they wished to return or between the home and the hospital to which they might have to go unless helped. When a psychiatrist became available, this concept was enlarged for Brook Lane Farm to include treatment. But the concept has not been lost. Some of those who have served in hospitals or who know "mild cases" who need retreat from the "irritating sources" still urge this concept. Recently Dr. Albert C. Voth, Psycholgist, Topeka State Hospital, suggested a similar possibility. As far as we know this is a relatively untried concept.

December 6, 1947, Newton, Kansas, Meeting

With so many of our church general hospitals in this central U.S. area, at this particular meeting considerable time was spent exploring possibilities of the psychiatric ward. Although recommended, none of the hospitals had immediate plans for complete psychiatric ward additions. The Bethel Hospital, Newton, Kansas, and the envisioned Elkhart, Indiana, hospital were perhaps farthest in their thinking.

The most immediate concern for attention appeared to be the chronic mentally ill and certain of the mentally deficient. At this meeting it was suggested that an investigation be made of the Harvey County Home possibility for this purpose.

Although this appeared to be the most pressing aspect of the mental illness problem, there was a strong conviction in the group that an over-all plan should be formulated for a long-range program to eventually provide the more complete service and training program. The possibility of a decentralized pattern with central administration was encouraged for further investigation.

In a general way the possibility presented was that of a series of farms within the general proximity to one city such as Newton, which has good general medical facilities. Each of these farms might presumably specialize on one of the following: (1) chronic mentally ill, (2) the acute mentally ill who need a strong therapy program, (3) "in-between" cases who might have been treated at a psychiatric ward or state hospital and who need little or no supervision, or "mild" cases who want a "retreat," and (4) training center for mentally deficient. Further decentralization to private homes was considered a possibility from several of these farms.

Reading 26

Report of the Mental Health Service Section to the Annual Meeting, March 17-18, 1950.

Brook Lane Farm

In October of 1948 Brook Lane Farm was dedicated and in December of 1948 it was licensed by the state of Maryland to receive mental patients. The first patient arrived at the hospital on January 21, 1949. Just one year later, the following statistics were compiled representing a record of patients cared for up until that time:

Number of patients admitted to Hospital	107
Number of patients discharged from Hospital	87
Average length of stay in Hospital (Patients now discharged)	34.95 da.
Average patient population per day	10.16
Denominational Status:	
Mennonite constituent groups	32
Others (Protestant & Catholic)	63
Professing no religion	12

The Brook Lane Farm concept is still that of giving

therapeutic treatment to both acute and mild cases of mental illness. We are now refusing all applicants that appear to be chronic cases.

The family-like relationship between patients and staff is being maintained in that they have their meals, devotions, and some social activities in common. It has, however, been necessary to destroy the illusion of complete intermingling of personnel and patients. The staff members must be spared continual contact with disturbed individuals. The essential discipline of hospitalized mental cases has made it necessary to establish an institutional aspect to the atmosphere of Brook Lane Farm. That this has been accomplished without loss of the feeling of Christian fellowship and security has been a major achievement of the past year.

West Coast Project

Arthur Jost, West Coast administrator, has been responsible for the Reedley Hospital development and has furnished this comprehensive report on activities. The interpretive and organizational aspects of the contemplated West Coast Mental Hospital program were emphasized during the first 9 months of the past fiscal year. Brother Orie Miller visited the constituency in April inspecting the forty-acre site located in Fresno and Tulare counties near Reedley California which was purchased in 1948. The building committee was appointed at that time. A further meeting in behalf of these interests was held in Portland, Oregon, to which brethren representing all of the Mennonite bodies in Oregon, Washington, and Idaho were invited. In a second visit to the West Coast in August, Brother Miller verified commitments regarding funds which needed to be proportionately allocated to the various Mennonite and Brethren in Christ groups in the West Coast constituency. The commitments were accepted with a deep sense of responsibility towards a project of this type which was to particularly serve the mentally ill among the brotherhood.

The June 7th Executive Committee meeting approved "Kings View Homes" as the name for the project since it is adjacent to the Kings River. A well qualified architect has completed detailed drawings and specifications for the first unit as well as a tentative master plan for the ultimate three-unit project. The first unit will provide thirty-two bed facilities. It comprises 8,499 sq. ft. of floor space and is of one-story reinforced concrete construction without basement. The windows are steel sash and the entire building is classified as a minimum restraint facility.

The ground-breaking service was held November 20 and was attended by approximately one thousand people mostly from the surrounding Mennonite constituency. P. C. Hiebert represented the Executive Committee and addressed the meeting.

Governor Earl Warren's personal representative and state commissioner for Mental Hygiene, Dr. Frank F. Tallman, also spoke, expressing a deep confidence in the motivation of the Mennonite constituency in such an undertaking.

Middle West

No site has been selected for this hospital to date. Dr. H. A. Fast continues to investigate suggested locations as they are brought to our attention. It has been felt that concentration of available resources in Kings View Homes' projects has left us without capacity of developing other facilities at this time. Midwest activity has therefore centered about the development of the Topeka center as a source of experience and constituency information in the psychiatric field. /A few weeks later Newton, Kansas was selected as the site for a mental health hospital. In March, 1954, Prairie View Hospital was opened./

* * *

Kings View was completed and began operation in early 1951. In December, 1952, the MCC Mental Health Section was incorporated as Mennonite Mental Health Services, Inc. This did not essentially change earlier personnel and responsibility arrangements, but created a separate corporation to hold the property of the new mental health institutions.

By 1954 all three hospitals were operating, and new plans were being formulated.

Reading 27

Report of Mental Health Section Director, May 27, 1954.

Since March 15th the three hospitals have been operating with a combined licensed capacity for 110 patients. At the present time approximately 75 patients are being cared for with prospects of expanding services to care for 100 patients within another six weeks. This does not take into account the very significant work being done with out-patients.

EAST CENTRAL AREA MENTAL HOSPITAL INTERESTS

On April the 3rd a group of 43 interested members of MCC constituent groups from the States of Ohio, Indiana, Illinois, and Michigan met at Goshen, Indiana. The complete report of that meeting is available to all Board members, but I want to draw your attention particularly to the meeting summary as embodied in Minute 10.

"Having met as representatives at Goshen, Indiana, April 3, 1954, of the various Mennonite groups in the Central States Area of Ohio, Indiana, Michigan and Illinois and having given consideration to the needs and possibilities for a Mennonite

Mental Hospital and Mental Health Service in this area, we find it to be our common mind that, while we are generally agreed as to the need and desirability of more Christian and professional care in the field of mental health, both in institutional, clinical and counselling service, we believe that further careful study should be given to all aspects of this question as a prerequisite to any decisions. Such a study should include the degree and character of the need, the possible and desirable type of institution and service to be established, the possible supply of Mennonite personnel, including the recruiting and the preparation of the same, as well, on the available financial costs and resources in our constituency."

* * *

The study suggested by the group meeting in Goshen was undertaken, and had two important results: 1) the recommendation that a facility be built in Elkhart County -- Oaklawn Psychiatric Center was opened in 1963 -- and 2) a broader study of MCC's administrative policy in its mental health program.

The final report, made in 1956, made proposals for several changes that would streamline the administrative pattern and begin a transition to greater local responsibility. Later, each center was incorporated separately, and each had its own board of directors. MCC retained only the power to appoint MMHS board members and approve the MMHS budget.

Reading 28

Findings of the MCC Mental Health Services Study Committee. Presented to Executive Committee Meeting, December 15, 1956.

From this study has emerged the following observations:

1. The MCC program in the area of Mental Health Services has been a pioneer venture. Worthwhile results have been achieved despite the professional inexperience of our people in this area of service.

2. One finds general agreement that we have a continuing ministry to perform to the mentally ill. Our people seem to be increasingly conscious of the needs in this area.

3. This new MCC program is being administered in recognition of the need for adaptation to changing needs and expanding experience. The MCC mental hospitals are to be encouraged to integrate their programs of services with the total needs and resources (medical, welfare, education, and constituency) of the region in which they serve. A marked trend in this direction is discernible in all three MCC institutions.

4. Feelings of uncertainty, dissatisfaction, and lack

of clarity have arisen in this initial period of pioneering.

5. The program appears to be growing too large, too widely distributed, and too complex for a highly centralized pattern of administration.

6. The committee's recommendations concerning administrative relationships have been outlined in the accompanying organizational chart....

* * *

By 1963, then, MCC had helped to establish four major mental health institutions. It played a minor role in the development of a few other church-related mental health institutions. A 1972 brochure published by MMHS, Inc. describes these four facilities.

Reading 29

"The Mennonite Mental Health Story." Published by Mennonite Mental Health Services, Inc., January 1, 1972.

Brook Lane Psychiatric Center

/Brook Lane/ was viewed as an "experimental project" which should help guide the establishment of other programs. Patients were to be of the "moderately-ill type", although this was later to include acute patients. The maximum stay was to be six months and the maximum cost $3.50 per day. A two-man Brook Lane advisory committee composed of Titus Books and Dr. Paul Nase was appointed, later in 1947 expanded to three with the addition of Walter Temple.

There was considerable agony in deciding the extent to which the farm home and buildings and CPS dormitories should be remodeled. Ultimately, in 1948, a new 23-bed hospital unit was constructed in addition to the necessary remodeling of existing buildings. MCC the first of that year also named Delvin Kirchhofer as administrator and secured the services of Dr. Helmut Prager of Baltimore as part-time psychiatrist and medical director. In January 1949, the first patients were admitted to Brook Lane Farm.

In 1959 the facility was incorporated as Brook Lane Farm Hospital, and responsibility for administration shifted essentially from MCC and its agency, Mennonite Mental Health Services (MMHS), to a Board of Directors. The facility was renamed Brook Lane Psychiatric Center in 1965 to express more adequately its growth and development as a community mental health center.

Through the years the facilities were expanded to include a total of 40 inpatient beds, an outpatient-administration building, a chapel-education facility, as well as residence and maintenance structures. Some twelve buildings now dot the twenty-five acre tract of land.

Kings View

Since opening its doors in 1951, Kings View has developed from a small mental hospital, mostly for the elderly disturbed and chronic patients, to a comprehensive mental health center providing multiple services of treatment and prevention. Under contract, Kings View provides all mental health services for five counties, with the exception of patients hospitalized in state mental hospitals. And even a significant number of these were returned to their home communities as local services were developed.

Prairie View

On March 15, 1954, Prairie View Hospital was opened to receive patients.

Dr. Harold Vogt, a clinical psychologist, provided professional leadership at the outset with Dr. Thomas Morrow serving as medical director on a part-time basis. Elmer Ediger, earlier chairman of the advisory committee, became administrator in 1957. For much of the time until 1961, Prairie View arranged with a private psychiatric group in Wichita to provide professional staff, but thereafter began building its own staff with Mitchell Jones, M.D., coming as the first full-time medical director.

The program made advances on numerous fronts. Facilities were expanded to include an activities building, an industrial therapy building and the original hospital was enlarged. An administrative and outpatient facility followed in 1967 and a recreational building in 1971. To help achieve local community responsibility, Prairie View has fostered the development of a citizen's organization, Community Mental Health Services, Inc., through which the local efforts have become more collaborative. Three area counties now contract for services and consultative and educational services are provided to community agencies and institutions.

Oaklawn Psychiatric Center

A new million-dollar plant, constructed on 22 acres of land at the edge but within the city limits of Elkhart, was ready for use in February 1963. The philosophy and program of operation focused on day treatment and outpatient services. Whereas the earlier MMHS mental hospitals began as inpatient psychiatric hospitals, Oaklawn was opened with no beds at all. Oaklawn does provide 24-hour care for those who require it in a community home program and by the inpatient care available at Elkhart General Hospital under supervision of Oaklawn's staff members. In recent years Oaklawn has admitted more patients to its programs than any other psychiatric facility in the state.

Programs of education and consultation are integral to

Oaklawn's way of working. The Oaklawn Foundation and Oaklawn Forum provide vehicles for developing community relations and support. The Center is available to the entire community, and five Indiana counties and one Michigan county are served through contractual relationships.

3.
Voluntary Service (VS)

The introductory paragraphs in quotation marks in this section are drawn from A Study of Mennonite Service Programs, prepared by Wilfred J. Unruh in 1967, in cooperation with the Institute of Mennonite Studies, Elkhart, Indiana.

Voluntary Service was the child of CPS, born during World War II. CPS men (and volunteer women) were giving vital services to society in other than military ways.

Reading 30

Unruh, A Study . . . Pp. A-89-90.

"The contribution of CPS rests at several levels: there was the exposure of men to human need; there was the vision of women to assist the men in their mission of mercy; there was the vision of leaders who saw in the dynamic of summer service and CPS the nucleus of a larger, longer term program of outreach; there was the high morale and good moral support that CPS men gave to the infant service effort; there were leaders for the young VS program who came out of the ranks of CPS; and there were the volunteers from CPS who stayed on to serve in voluntary service, as at Gulfport where about one-half the men stayed on for some time to assist in a transitional period. A more subtle, but probably more significant contribution of CPS to the emerging voluntary service movement was the way in which men of vision and action were brought together in the catalyst of CPS work. In the area of leadership particularly the focusing of creative minds at MCC headquarters and in the CPS project leadership served to stimulate the search of a relevant ministry in the contemporary community."

Reading 31

Unruh, A Study . . . P. 85.

"The years 1945 gave rise to many questions and observations. Why not continue this service program in post-war years? What will MCC's mandate be if conscription were to end? Several men participated in five or six discussions concerning what to do with the young people of the Mennonite Church who would want to serve after CPS days. This group presented a five page memorandum to MCC administrators in the late 1940's

"The statement these men made was informal; nevertheless, it was to become the core of reference for the emerging program. One of the group's proposals was 'the establishment of an administrative section in Akron to succeed CPS which might be called the 'Christian Public Service Section', 'Voluntary Service Section', or 'Mennonite Youth Section'. Orie O. Miller's immediate preference was 'Voluntary Service Section' and so it came to be.' (Elmer Ediger, report-winter, 1959 follows):

"There has been considerable agitation on the part of college women for some outlet in the form of service which would be comparable to that which the CPS boys are now giving in the mental hospitals. When it was learned that women workers were needed in these hospitals, the girls became interested in a summer unit for college girls. This desire on the part of the girls to provide needed service and to enroll in relief training classes was conveyed to officials of the schools at Bluffton College and also at Goshen College. Officials of the schools, in turn, approached the MCC, with the result that a decision was reached to establish two units for summer vacation relief training of such college women as may want to avail themselves of the opportunity. These units are to be located at the Ypsilanti State Hospital, Ypsilanti, Michigan, and at the State Hospital for Mental Diseases at Howard, Rhode Island. It was known that both institutions would welcome the services which college women could give during the summer months."

/These words describe the earliest specific actions which in time led to organized MCC voluntary service programs./

"In 1946 two significant events occurred. A long-term unit was established at Gulfport, Mississippi, and a set of standards and aims for the VS program was created. Twelve units were organized by MCC during the first four years of its VS department.

"Migrant workers, camps, mental hospitals and institutions for juvenile delinquents were areas in which VS'ers participated. Each VSer received $10.00 per month; the remainder of the money that would ordinarily have been received was sent to MCC in an effort to make the program largely self-supporting."

Reading 32

<u>Report on Standards and Plans for a Possible Voluntary Services Program during 1947. Submitted to Special Meeting of MCC, October 31, 1946.</u>

<u>Why Such a Program</u>

We live in a world of need and confusion. A growing consciousness of the suffering, the hopelessness, and the evil of a war-torn world has caused us to become restless in our own favored situation. We cannot help but contrast the need with that of our own spiritual opportunities and our abundance of material wealth which we so often take for granted. The realization of the love of God and the fruits of His blessings constrain us to give ourselves to a greater service of love during peace as well as war time.

The Kingdom of God requires that all of its citizens serve with their time and talents. Many thus rightly find their place of service in the field and factory, in the office and in school. Our total task however requires that some give full time service in extending the work of the church. Certainly there should also be a place for short term service through the church by those young people who have such a period of time to contribute.

Our Christian young people are taught to give and to serve in the name of Christ, yet so often the opportunity for challenging service is unavailable or the field is uncharted and a practical expression of love fails to come to fruition. It is a privilege of the church to endeavor to connect this service potential with the existing needs. For an effective utilization of this offering of time and talent it would seem desirable to plan a well balanced voluntary service program.

War sufferers' relief, summer service units, and in some respects CPS have provided just such opportunities. With peacetime at hand it is felt that there will be continued willingness to give time and talents to minister to those who are less fortunate than we. Voluntary service can grow to meet this general purpose. Jointly Mennonite and Brethren in Christ groups can experiment with various projects and needs and thus be helpful to individual groups who are planning their own program. The MCC as servant of the churches should endeavor to provide a continuous program of opportunities that will supplement rather than compete with what individual groups may sponsor.

Set forth below are specific aims of such a program, the standards of volunteers who would qualify to serve, and standards for voluntary service projects.

<u>Aims of Voluntary Services</u>

1. To provide channels of Christian Service for young people who have a period of a year or less to contribute at some cost to themselves.

2. To provide a means of testifying more widely to the Gospel and its way of love and non-resistance.

3. To provide projects that will help alleviate human need, tension, and spiritual confusion, and which will use able volunteers in service respectable to those served, the worker, and our constituencies.

4. To provide an experience of internship in Christian service--in finding a purer service motivation, a more effective witness, a greater sense of church, and the will of God in each one's own life.

5. To provide in voluntary service for the Christian citizen an opportunity to express his appreciation for the material blessings, religious and other national liberties, and to contribute to the well being of our nation.

6. To provide through voluntary service an opportunity to gain a fuller realization of the soul-sick world and a clearer understanding of the "good news" with the hope that more individuals will be constrained by the love of Christ to give themselves to full time ministry or missionary service.

Standards of volunteers:

1. A voluntary worker should be a Christian, desirous of serving wherever possible in the name of his Lord and Saviour.

2. A voluntary worker should be willing to contribute his services without regard to financial remuneration.

3. A voluntary worker should be desirious of growing in the life of love--in giving up of self, in finding the will of God, in developing habits of prayerful devotion, and in disciplining self strictly to the way of love and nonresistance in all personal and group relationships.

4. A voluntary worker should give evidence of good standing with his church and should represent it worthily.

5. A voluntary worker living with representatives of various church groups should manifest a willingness and effort to respect another's convictions and to avoid such practices and attitudes as would be a stumbling block to others.

Standards of Voluntary Service Projects

1. To provide projects: (a) Within institutions that will reach those hungry for Christian love, that will relieve labor shortages, give needed supplemental service, or raise standards of treatment particularly in institutions which serve the handicapped and those shut off from society; (b) Where volunteer time and talent can be shared with a local community in helping to meet their problems of disease such as hookworm or tuberculosis, problem of juvenile delinquency, poverty, and the very common problem of churches--a lack of spiritual vitality and evidence of Christian love; (d) To assist our local churches or centers in preparing material aid for relief and missions.

2. To render in such a way a total group Christian service that God will be glorified and that individuals are brought closer to his love and the knowledge of his saving Gospel. In general it may be a service in deed more than

word but there should always be encouragement and opportunities provided for individuals and group evangelical witnessing. Voluntary service projects are not a substitute for missionary work but an aspect of it which is preparatory and supplemental to his primary task of the church. If at all possible the longer term projects should have arrangements with one of our constituent conferences or with a local evangelical church which will help bring the broader Christian service testimony to fruition in the individuals served.

3. To have a balanced program of projects which provide as much as possible for utilization of the varying individual talents and abilities--manual, teaching, recreational, nursing, homemaking and other interests of a general nature.

4. To avoid exploitation of volunteer labor. Where remuneration has normally been or should be given the employer is expected to pay for services rendered. Strictly speaking, to be on the volunteer basis means to serve on subsistence allowance. Short term service workers as in mental hospitals will be encouraged to contribute from their earnings to other projects. In general the longer term workers on volunteer basis will contribute their earnings beyond subsistence to other voluntary service projects or another worthy cause.

5. To cooperate with a government agency where adviseable to initiate, demonstrate, or to perform a worthwhile task which has a particular potential for a group witness. Freedom for group and individual religious life and witness should be a prerequisite of any cooperating arrangement.

6. To use volunteers as a group or provide for periodic group experiences to nurture the purest Christian motivation and to help provide a sense of church purpose and program. Provisions for a strong spiritual undergirding and atmosphere are all important to render the individual and group service in the name of Christ.

7. To provide adequate leadership for the project and the religious and educational life of the unit. This is essential and will determine to a great extent how completely the aims and standards of the total program can be realized.

* * *

From 1948 to 1951 MCC also operated VS work camps in Europe.

Reading 33

Excerpt, Voluntary Service Report--Report on Summer in Europe, by Elmer Ediger. Executive Committee Meeting, September 25, 1948.

Aims: 1. To direct summer V.S. units in Germany
2. To plan for continuing European V.S. program

3. To observe from personal experience the MCC program in Europe

Itinerary:

I left New York on June 3 together with the student group. A short time was spent with the students in England. Fortunately I was able to meet Atlee Beechy and J. N. Byler at Amsterdam and proceed with them in a brief visit to MCC units in Germany and France, including the two proposed V.S. sites for the summer. The Basel conference which followed was an excellent orientation to European Mennonitism, and the director's conference was an excellent follow-up of the brief tour. The week before the opening of Ronneburg was spent in that area making preparations. I was at Ronneburg for the entire period with the exception of one week which was used for the two-fold purpose of visiting the Hamburg unit and to investigate the Ruhr and Bielefeld areas for possible V.S. projects. After the Ronneburg unit ended two conferences followed in immediate succession, which were very timely in terms of summarizing our experience and giving us an over-all view of youth service in Europe. The Neustadt conference was aimed to bring together the German Mennonite leaders, the German Mennonite youth who had been in V.S. this summer and MCC workers concerned with the future of European V.S. The Stuttgart conference was called by the American Military Government for all agencies operating units in the American Zone this summer. This gave us all insight of the philosophy and experience of eleven other groups and thus helped to clarify our own purposes. Several days were then spent in Basel trying to bring together the V.S. plans for Europe. A trip to Italy followed investigation of V.S. possibilities. It was helpful in getting a feel of the Waldensian church and their desire for our cooperation with them.

The Neustadt conference with the German leadership was significant. It was felt that before proceeding with the continuing V.S. program in Europe we should make certain such a program is welcome by the German Mennonite leadership. The young people who had been in the units did an excellent and enthusiastic job of interpreting the units to the leadership. The leadership group, after a brief counsel among themselves, encouraged us definitely to go ahead with the program and they would help in getting the young people acquainted with the program. In fact, they had so many suggestions for how to do a better job of publicizing that we were almost astounded.

* * *

During the years of 1950-1954, war had a direct effect on the VS program. The Korean conflict made it evident that military conscription would continue. The influx of men seeking to serve their time in approved alternate service created additional motivation to seek church related service. Readings 34 and 35 show MCC's response to this problem. Again, during these four years twelve units were opened. Others were teminated as unit purposes were fulfilled and members' terms ended. In 1953 the Canadian MCC regional office assumed responsibiltiy for Canadian VS projects.

Reading 34

Message from the Mennonite Central Committee to its Constituency Regarding Voluntary Service by our Young People in the Light of the Present Emergency. Adopted at MCC Special Meeting, October 7, 1950.

We, the delegated representatives of the Mennonite and Brethren in Christ constituent groups cooperating in the Mennonite Central Committee, particularly in its Peace Section, having met in special session in Chicago, Illinois, on October 7, 1950, have carefully considered our responsibility as non-resistant Christians in the light of the present emergency in the nation and in the world, having particularly in mind the existing international tensions, such as those between the western nations and Soviet Russia, the actual warfare in the Far East, and the decision to greatly expand the military strength of the nation through a military draft, increased military expenditures and the direction of increased production and manpower to military ends. While it is true that at present conscientious objectors are deferred by law and no other compulsory participation in the military program or its support has yet been required, we believe that the Christian response to the needs and challenges of the present hour dare not be primarily determined by the dictates of the state nor the pressure of the society in which we live but by the principles of faith and life derived from the Word of God and the Gospel which control our lives and dictate our behaviour.

After earnest and prayerful consideration we send the following message to our constituent groups with the request that each review the issues involved and respond to the MCC Executive Secretary with a clear group mandate and commitment so that our MCC administration may have the necessary information and directives to serve the constituency as is desired, as well as a solid basis of support.

Message

1. Believing that those who would follow Christ in full discipleship in the way of peace and love are at all times called to serve the needs of the world both spiritual and

material in the name and spirit of Christ but particularly so in a time of world distress and emergency, such as the present, we call upon our churches, and particularly all young men and women, to enlarge their ministry of service with a deepened sense of responsibility. This should mean more persons in service, longer periods of service, and more service to those outside of our fold in our communities, our country, and the needy areas of the world beyond. It does not mean service taken up under pressure without a clear and sincere Christian purpose, nor the abandonment without call of present, significant Christian work or preparation for greater usefulness in service. It does mean that all of our young people, however, whose family and life circumstances permit, particularly between the ages of 19 to 25, and older, should seriously face the question before God whether they should not now offer themselves for a substantial period of direct special service, both to meet the needs of their fellowmen and to give a further witness for Christ and His Gospel. It will mean that significant work projects must be provided by the church which will of themselves be both valuable in service and give good room for Christian witness in the life and spirit of the worker as well. Christian love and redemptive action must find expression in our ministry of service now more than ever before in view of the spirit of the times which emphasizes the use of force and war in attempts to solve current problems.

2. If we agree upon our response to the present situation as set forth above, then we must provide for an expanded program of voluntary service now. This means also that it must become clear what we wish the MCC to undertake for our various groups in this field. For the past several years, at the request of the constituency, the MCC has served us by (1) pioneering and experimenting, as well as by (2) providing service projects under its own administration for those volunteers who come to it, within the limits of financial ability. However, the financial support from the constituency has not come forth in the expected and needed amounts, so that there is actually a large and growing deficit. This state of affairs cannot continue. It is, therefore, essential for each constituent group to state clearly (1) whether it will confirm the existing mandate to the MCC in respect to voluntary service or change it and (2) whether it wishes the MCC to assume all or part of the expanded program of voluntary service which will come if the response suggested in Point 1 is agreed to and (3) whether it will give corresponding financial support. We believe also that if the several groups, or some of them, plan to undertake for their young people all or part of the expanded program themselves a goodly measure of brotherly cooperation both together and with the MCC program will be both desirable and necessary in view of the total situation

obtaining in this country, and that the groups will desire to give such cooperation.

3. It will also be necessary for our constituent groups to give a clear commitment to the MCC as to the financial support for any program they request the MCC to undertake. Current reports show that, even including the net income from such maintenance projects as state mental hospitals, etc., afford, the cost for a well-balanced and varied service program is now running at about $25.00 per worker-month, including overhead administrative cost, travel to points of service, worker maintenance, etc. If workers are to be used in foreign projects this cost will naturally go higher. We, therefore, request our several constituent groups to indicate how they believe the MCC Voluntary Service budget should be financed and what they themselves propose to do.

4. Statements from our groups as to the types of service projects they desire will be very helpful to the MCC administration in planning its future voluntary service program.

In conclusion, we then call upon our constituent groups to make clear their own attitudes on the issues which our groups now face and which we have outlined in this message, and to set forth the mandate each wishes to give to the MCC for the future voluntary service program, together with a definite commitment to financial support. It should be understood that this message does not deal with the question of alternative service in case of future conscription of C.O.'s, although, without doubt, what we do in voluntary service may help us to meet the issues involved in conscription if and when it comes. Nor should our young people enter into voluntary service now assuming that this will necessarily displace future conscripted service.

This message is being sent to each official group representative in the MCC Peace Section with the request that it be transmitted to the proper body for consideration and appropriate action at an early date."

Reading 35

<u>Unruh, A Study</u>... Pp. A-101-102.

The draft law revisions affecting C.O. men were first approved in early 1952. The first men did not report for service until after mid year. Thus planning for the service program in early 1952 continued to be a frustrating necessity. As the draft laws were defined it became clear that the MCC could not conceivably include all the Mennonite and Brethren in Christ men in its VS program. Soon the pattern of the "earning, independent 1-W alternative service worker" was seen as the predominant service choice for C.O. men.

In a September 27, 1952, session of the Committee on

Advice and Control set as its objective to provide a service program that might use from 80-100 long term workers annually, and that those 1-W men serving in paid assignments in MCC institutions be secured through channels other than the VS office.

There was some thought given to the direction of the program's emphasis in 1955-56. Prior to 1955 much of the emphasis had been on mental health. According to a statement in the 1955 workbook, the program's emphasis turned to juvenile delinquency. . .

During the years 1955 to 1966, the VS program entered at least one new area each year, with the exception of 1962. These years seemed to show an emphasis on cultures different than North American. The problems of race and poverty were also encountered. . . .

First teachers and medical personnel were sent to Newfoundland in 1954. . . .

Haiti. . . received their first MCC workers in 1958. Community development and hospital work /were/ the projects in this small country.

The Dominican Republic, Guatemala, Mexico and St. Lucia were the 'different' cultures VS entered in the /early 1960's/. Community development /was/ the aim in the Dominican Republic and Mexico. Guatemala and St. Lucia . . . received VS teachers.

The Hoopa Indian Reservation in California, inner-city work in Atlanta and rural development in Appalachia and Mississippi /were/ projects which also joined the growing MCC 'family' in these . . . years. Hospital work (supplying doctors and nurses) and community development /were/ the primary aspects in Hoopa and Applachia. . .

* * *

Readings 36 and 37 illustrate some of the developments in the VS program during these years.

Reading 36

Executive Committee Meeting Minutes, November 18-19, 1960.

a. Minute 6 MEXICO — Moved and passed that another trip be made to Mexico to survey the needs carefully in preparation for the establishment of a VS unit along lines approved in minute 9 of the May 26, 1960 and other related services with full report and recommendation to be given to the VS Advisory Committee.

b. Minute 7 SOUTH — The Committee reviewed its previous actions regarding the establishment of a VS unit in the South. Elmer Neufeld was in attendance and presented the actions the MCC Peace Section has taken and outlined some tentative plans to proceed. The discussion led to the following action:

Moved and passed that the VS Advisory Committee confirm its previous action to supplement a proposed Peace Section project in the South with a VS unit of 4-6 workers. The Peace Section is requested to be mindful of this interest, and encouraged to make service project suggestions. If and when the Peace Section is able to locate, the VS administration shall visit the project to assess service opportunities with report and recommendation to be brought to the VS Advisory Committee. To initiate this project, VS is prepared to assume one-half support of a worker for a period of one year with a maximum of $4,000.

Reading 37

VS Advisory Committee Minutes, April 12, 1961.

9. PROGRAM REPORT: A brief program review was presented by Claude Boyer and by Edgar Stoesz in the absence of Harvey Taves.

10. MEXICO: Moved and passed to plan an initial unit of 6-8 including leader, Stanely Pankratz and wife, for initial program development as follows: (a) Two single men for seconding to Heifer Project need. (b) Two single men for Mazahua area agriculture services program development similar to Haiti (Petit Goave) or Greece unit approach. (c) Two single teacher qualified women or married couple (B.S. in Education plus preferably Spanish language for 1961 Norman, Oklahoma, Linguistic training) and assignment to Mazahua tribes area adult literacy program. (This subject to Wycliff formal endorsement and assurance of cooperation as experiment.)

To have the initial unit residence base be in a county seat town of Mazahua area 100 miles S.W. of Mexico City.

To refer the Tlaxiaco need suggestion from Wycliff to Elkhart and in terms of Ray Horst expressed interest.

To review the program for further development in from 6-12 months.

11. NEWFOUNDLAND: The following action was taken in response to several needs that have arisen out of the Newfoundland projects. (a) Moved and passed that MCC donate a good used piano to the Twillingate Regional High School to assist in the development of a music program in the school. (b) Moved and passed that MCC enlarge its assistance in Newfoundland to include agricultural services and religious training through the United Church of Canada subject to the availability of necessary personnel, proper invitation from

sponsoring organizations and adequate structuring of the proposed project.

12. THE SOUTH: The committee approved the following recommendations with the stipulation that the VS administration visit the projects during the summer. (1) That we accept the invitation of the Wheat Street Baptist Church in Atlanta, Georgia, to have a Summer Service unit serve in their program. (2) That we accept the invitation of the South Street Community Center, Nashville, Tennessee, to have a unit of from 4-6 serve in the Community Center program...

* * *

Along with opening new units and exploring new possibilities there was the need for constant re-evaluation and scrutiny of the VS program. In 1962, VS administrators spent a considerable amount of time looking at the program as it was then. During this time, conferences were held between VS administrators, between VS administrators and constituents, and between the various conference groups. The result was a restatement of objective, personnel requirements, etc. This revision was not a whole new program but rather updating the present one.

Reading 38

Program of Mennonite Central Committee Voluntary Service. Presented to Annual Meeting, January 18-19, 1963.

The Mennonite Central Committee Voluntary Service program came into being in 1946 when program objectives and project criteria were developed by Mennonite Civilian Public Service leaders who felt that a voluntary program would be of far greater significance than a compulsory program such as we experienced in World War II. Between 1946 and 1962, approximately 1,600 young people have served for one or two years in MCC Voluntary Service. Additionally almost 3,000 summers were contributed through the summer service channel of the Voluntary Service program.

In 1962, the Executive Committee of MCC felt it would be useful to restate the objectives, project criteria, relationships to constituent groups, and personnel requirements of MCC VS. This statement is the result of many conferences with the MCC Executive Committee, constitutent groups' VS leaders, conference offices, and MCC members. In general, the statement does not represent a wholly new program emphasis, but rather updates and states current program practices. On December 14, 1962, the MCC Executive Committee acted to recommend this statement to the annual meeting for adoption as the basis for the MCC Voluntary Service Section.

Program of Mennonite Central Committee
VOLUNTARY SERVICE
A. MCC VOLUNTARY SERVICE OBJECTIVES

1. To provide channels of Christian service which will utilize well-motivated young people who have some time to contribute, at some cost to themselves, regardless of specialized talents or level of academic training.
2. To help others, both directly and indirectly, to establish a personal relationship with God.
3. To help alleviate human suffering on all levels--following the example of Christ's ministry.
4. To promote a spirit of self-sacrifice and stewardship both in terms of time and money.
5. To benefit the participants. While the primary purpose of the Voluntary Service experience is to help others, it is also intended to provide: (a) An educational internship experience for its participants who may be searching for the will of God in their lives. (b) A supporting community which will permit participants to develop and mature in a Christian environment and experience a fuller sense of church fellowship and responsibility. (c) Another opportunity for inter-Mennonite and, in some cases, interchurch experience which leads to greater understanding between groups, an identification with the larger Christian cause and contribute to a united Christian witness.
6. To gain within our constituency a more realistic and compassionate understanding of the world in which we live through having young people become personally involved with the spiritual and physical needs of others.
7. To prepare young people, as they return to their home churches after a term of service, to strengthen and enrich the congregations through their active participation or to make themselves available to serve in the mission, pastoral, and institutional work of the church on a more permanent basis.

B. PERSONNEL QUALIFICATIONS

(Same as those to be approved for all MCC personnel as printed in the new edition of the Handbook.)

C. PROJECT CRITERIA

1. A clearly demonstrated need that is challenging and within the capacity of the volunteers.
2. Mutual agreement must be reached on work assignments, housing, and financial arrangements before a project can be approved. Normally the receiving agency is expected to provide work supervision, unit housing, and pay to MCC for such services according to ability with prevailing wage being the maximum.
3. A willingness on the part of the receiving agency to respect our Mennonite beliefs and allow the unit to carry

out, both within and without the unit, a religious life program which is mutually agreed upon as appropriate under the circumstances.

4. A broad variety of work opportunities which will challenge and accommodate all properly motivated young people.

5. Eligibility for Selective Service approval for 1-W employment wherever possible.

6. Exploration of and pioneering in new locations and types of VS; the benefit of which can also be made available to conference sponsored VS programs.

D. ADMINISTRATION

1. As part of the approved MCC program, the VS administration is directly responsible to the MCC through the MCC Executive Committee and its Executive Secretary. The MCC members, both in the United States and Canada, are responsible for relating the MCC VS program to their respective constituency including VS programs where they exist.

2. Project administration is the responsibility of the VS staff with the assistance of the MCC service departments (Personnel Office, Treasurer's Office, and Information Services).

3. Participants are generally to be assigned in groups of at least four members who are to be organized as a unit with one member service as leader.

Unruh, A Study... "MCC's VS department has completed twenty years of service /in 1967/. A total of 1,305 persons have served during this period. As various areas of concern have been recognized - mental illness, juvenile delinquency, poverty, race - the VS department moved to meaningful participation. As new areas and needs become known, the VS department will continue to explore, experiment and research - and then move to serve 'In the Name of Christ'."

* * *

The following readings illustrate some of the MCC VS programs and issues faced as it developed in the 1970's.

Reading 39

Canadian VS Report to Executive Committee Meeting, March 13-14, 1969, and to MCC Canada Executive Committee Meeting, April 11-12, 1969.

Newfoundland

Considering the fact that 23 VSers are in their first year in Newfoundland, it is perhaps to be expected that we do have what seems to be our share of adjustment difficulties. Three teachers have for various reasons found the adjustments too difficult to make and have returned home from their assignments. Two others are remaining in Newfoundland perhaps primarily because we are attempting to stand by them in a fairly consistent manner. I believe the primary reason for our difficulties is the rather dramatic shift in a few instances which we have made to the more isolated areas in Newfoundland. Our experiences of this year will assist us considerably in evaluating personnel for the assignments which seem to demand fairly major adjustments.

From March 15-28, Doug Snyder is visiting a number of our teachers in Newfoundland. He has had several years of experience in teaching in northern Ontario among the Indians. This background will assist him in giving counsel in the teaching situations and he is also encouraged to fulfill a pastoral counselling function.

On April 25 an educational representative from Newfoundland will meet in Akron with several of us to discuss both the present teaching assignments in addition to making tentative assignments for approximately a dozen new teachers for this Fall.

In 1970 for the first time we are calling all of our Newfoundland VSers together to St. John's for a two-day retreat on June 25-26. It is hoped that the newly appointed teachers can join this group and thus provide a more complete orientaion through interaction with those who have spent at least one year or two in Newfoundland.

Toronto Service Program

Our Toronto VSers are kept busy in assisting families directly and indirectly in meeting the needs of children both in the home and the larger communities. At Warden Woods there is evidence that more families are becoming aware of the services which our VSers render and there is evidence that a confidence is growing in the program.

Since Toronto also has a number of economically depressed areas, especially with respect to housing needs, I will be giving a brief separate report on how the Toronto Service Program may become constructively involved in meeting some of this need.

Thompson Day Nursery, Manitoba

I have just recently visited our Thompson Day Nursery and find that the girls are doing a commendable job. Eight to a dozen pre-school children are cared for while mothers whose husbands have deserted them work to make a living. In some cases it is a matter of brief illness in the home while in still others there is simply an inability of a mother to handle her own children.

Woodlands School

One of the two fellows at Woodlands School in New

Westminster, British Columbia has returned from his assignment since the initiative and leadership required to work with these residents was more than he was able to produce. The fellow who remains there is doing a very fine job in the recreational education program.

Menno Home, Saskatchewan

We have assigned one VSer to this MCC (Saskatchewan) operated home for retardates. He is working in the woodwork shop and already reports thus far concerning his work and person have been positive. They are requesting a second person as general aid to residents as soon as we can supply him.

Lord Selkirk Park Inter-Faith Center

This project was described in our November Executive Committee Meeting. We have not yet secured personnel for this project, but negotiations are underway at the present time.

New Projects

Several projects in the province of Ontario have been developing over the past six months to a year. In most of these Doug Snyder, MCC (Ontario) director, would relate rather closely to VSers who would be assigned.

Oshawa Men's Hostel

A. Nature of Project

This is an outgrowth of the ideas of the London Rescue Mission with its developing emphasis on rehabilitation of derelicts. A graduate of the London Rescue Mission serves as the director for this Oshawa Hostel.

The Mennonite Mission and Service Board, representing the Ontario General Conference, Stirling Avenue, Western Ontario Mennonite and Ontario Mennonite conferences sponsor the Hostel with a local Oshawa Board of Directors representing the Anglican, Roman Catholic, Pentecostal, United, and Baptist Churches of Oshawa. The Oshawa City Welfare coordinator also sits on this Board. The rehabilitation program includes referrals to alcoholic and drug research foundation, mental health clinic and Alcoholic Anonymous.

B. Workers Needed

The type of workers needed for this program will be provided in more detail to the Personnel Office. Much of the training for these persons will be provided on the job under the supervision of the Hostel director. The volunteer would spend at least one week at the London Rescue Mission as part of his orientation.

Since Oshawa is not far from Toronto it would be proposed

that any Oshawa VSers could relate on a fairly regular basis to the Toronto Service Program personnel.

C. It is recommended that the Oshawa Men's Hostel be approved as a project for MCC VS assignments as negotiated with the Personnel Office with the initial financial arrangements being such that Oshawa will provide room and board and Voluntary Service expenses to Mennonite Central Committee who in turn deal with the VSer on the regular voluntary service arrangement.

Youth Probation Services

MCC (Ontario) has investigated in some detail the present program in Ontario to rehabilitate prisoners as well as what MCC (Ontario) could add to such services.

MCC (Ontario) has decided to focus its attention on ministering to youth who is serving a probation term. Prison authorities and other services in Ontario seem ready to cooperate in MCC's ministry to young people who, for various reasons, have come in conflict with the law, have been apprehended, and sentenced to a penal institution. There seems to be strong agreement that the best possible time to help the young offender is in the probation period, before he has come into contact with "profession" criminals which are found in the various penal institutions in the province.

The Probabion Department has indicated its openness to MCC volunteers. It would provide an orientation for VSers and also supervision on the assignments. They would provide regular reports to MCC concerning the work of the volunteers. A designated person in the Probation Department would be the one to whom the volunteer reports and with whom he counsels on a regular basis. The Probation Department would also provide the necessary transportation for the volunteer.

A detailed description of workers needed would be communicated to the Personnel Office. There are obviously certain qualifications necessary, one of these being the ability to absorb hostility. The persons would probably need to be from 20 to 30 years of age.

MCC (Ontario) is approaching this as a pilot project with a two-year term in mind. At the end of this period the project would be thoroughly evaluated and the decision made concerning any further development.

Reading 40

VS Report to Executive Committee Meeting, December 16-17, 1971

MEADOW LAKE, SASKATCHEWAN: The beginning of the MCC VS program in Meadow Lake has been quite disturbing to the Mennonite community there. Tim McEvoy, our only volunteer in Meadow Lake, is a Roman Catholic with an Anabaptist commitment and understanding. The Metis youth with MCC financial support and Tim's assistance have rented a building for a youth center. Some feel that this program is not "evangelical" and question Tim's Christianity. He is asking some very penetrating questions about how an MCC volunteer should be involved in church building. I would like this committee to seriously consider his questions. The volume of correspondence would be too great to share with you but I am including with this report a copy of Tim's November 16 letter.

Reading 41

Excerpt, VS Report, September 26-27, 1973.

INDIAN PROGRAM - For this year, we set aside $15,000 from the VS fund balance to use in various Indian programs. Approximately $1,000 of this amount was used to bring Mennonite Indian leaders to the seminar on Indian Americans which was held in Washington in early May. The Findings Committee from this seminar suggested the urgent need to educate the Mennonite constituency about the current mood and situation of Indian Americans. Emma LaRoque, a Metis Cree Indian from Alberta, is a student at Goshen College in journalism and communications. Emma was available for the summer, so Ray Horst and I developed a cooperative program to use her services. Emma spent several weeks with the Choctaw Indian community near Philadelphia, Mississippi, several weeks in Rapid City, South Dakota, and completed her summer writing assignment by visiting the Navajo and Hopi Indians in Arizona and New Mexico. She visited the Elkhart office, MCC office, GC office in Newton and the MB headquarters in Hillsboro. She has written interpretive articles about the VS program and the Indian situations in the various places where she visited. MCC covered the cost of her transportation from place to place and in addition is granting her a $1,200 scholarship toward her final year at Goshen College. Local expenses and accommodations were covered by the various conference offices in the areas where she visited. All of the articles which Emma produced have been sent to MCC News Service for distribution. While many of the articles written were not "hard news" items, nonetheless Emma has produced some very interesting and informative materials. This has been a growing and enriching experience for Emma and the Church in working with a minority person in this type role.

The seminar on Indian Americans brought us in contact with many of the national offices of various Indian organications. The Indian Legal Information Development Service, which publishes the Legislative Review, contacted us for assistance in distributing this publication. Two copies of this publication were printed but they did not have funds for mailing. The Legislative Review is sent to each of the Indian tribes as well as a number of interested Senators and Representatives. It is one of the best compilations of laws affecting the Indians in the U.S. We supplied a one-time grant of $311.50 to underwrite the mailing of two issues of the Legislative Review. There are several agencies in Washington that are in desperate need of volunteer personnel to assist them in research and writing. We would very much like to assign volunteers to several of these agencies if volunteers become available.

4. Mennonite Disaster Service (MDS)

Reading 42

"Mennonites: A Brief History of Mennonite Disaster Service," from Handbook for Mennonite Disaster Service Volunteers, by Vernon R. Wiebe, 1960.

Mennonite Disaster Service began as a practical application of the biblical injunction to "Love the Lord thy God with all thy heart...and thy neighbor as thyself." Through the four centuries of their existence Mennonites have always practiced the commandment wherever there was a need. But it was the demands of specialization of the mid-twentieth century which dictated the formal organization as we have it today.

Mennonite Disaster Service, hereafter referred to as MDS, can be traced to a young married couples' Sunday School picnic in the summer of 1950. The young couples of the Pennsylvania Mennonite Church and Hesston College Church had gathered for joint fellowship. In the course of the gathering a concern was raised about the practical outworking of a concern for their neighbors. A committee was formed and statement of concern and willingness to serve was sent to MCC and the South Central Conference of the Mennonite Church.

During the fall and winter of that year a Mennonite Service Organization was begun in the two Hesston congregations. John Diller was appointed the coordinator of the group.

The first opportunity for service came on May 17, 1951, when a call for help to sandbag the Little Arkansas River in Wichita attracted the attention of the organization. Volunteers were sent and the Mennonite Service Organization was in business. That same night John Diller called the Eden Church of the General Conference and the Christian Welfare Workers of the Church of God in Christ Mennonite and inter-Mennonite cooperation in disaster service was born.

In 1951 was the year of the big rains in Kansas and Mennonite congregations in the state found many opportunities to serve. Many of the Mennonite churches sent volunteers to help in the flood areas of Marion, Florance, Topeka, and Kansas City.

That fall an MCC unit moved into Topeka to aid disaster victims. Esley Schmidt of the Tabor Mennonite Church was appointed director of the unit.

In the meantime John Diller had been instructed by his

Mennonite Service Organization to inquire of MCC whether volunteers could supplement the unit program at Topeka.

The plan for service became crystallized during the Christmas holidays of 1951. Esley Schmidt had come home for the vacation. During his stay he inquired of John Diller as to when the Hesston MSO could send volunteers. The Topeka Unit had been waiting for help.

Better organization was necessary. A meeting was called on December 26 at the Hesston Manufacturing Plant in Hesston to set up a basis for sending volunteers to help at Topeka. John Diller was appointed the coordinator of this program. The other two churches' representatives did not feel that they could speak for their whole body. It is significant to note the wisdom of this first pattern of organization. It has served the organization well and is still the organizational pattern, practically without amendment.

The disaster committee was given three directives which continue to be operative today. (1) The committee was not to take the place of present relief committees, brotherhoods, and service organizations. (2) In the event of a major disaster, the committee was empowered to investigate the needs and avenues of service immediately, and to report to each local organization, coordinating the local organizations into the total program. (3) The committee was not to be a money raising organization.

Immediately after adjournemnt the committee met and selected Peter J. Dyck as chairman and John Diller as secretary-treasurer. Arrangements were made to send a representative into the Arkansas storm area and contact proper officials to determine what is needed, either men or other material. And so MDS was born in service!

* * *

In May, 1952, MCC began to discuss what its role might be in the overall disaster relief effort.

Reading 43

MCC Memorandum from Ray Horst to Orie O. Miller, May 2, 1952.

In addition to /the/ specific concern for the unit to be sent into /the / Arkansas area, our group also discussed the possibility of establishing a regular disaster service program. After considerable discussion it was felt that it would be advisable for MCC to have one person on the regular MCC VS staff who would direct this type of service. This person should be available to move into any area struck by a disaster and organize a Mennonite unit to assist during the emergency and direct the rehabilitation period. This person should be able to serve in the following capacities:

1. Serve as official contact man for MCC and the Mennonite groups in dealing with the Red Cross, community officials, other welfare agencies, and the individuals to be served.

2. Should be able to serve and be project foreman and direct the project to be undertaken by the service unit.

3. Should be able to serve as unit leader for the group serving in the area. In this respect he should be able to give direction to the religious and recreational life of the group during the period that they are in the area.

4. He should be officially responsible to give reports on the project for release through our church papers.

In addition to the responsibilities which such an individual would have at the site of an emergency, he should be available for contact with our various church groups and different Mennonite communities. This would enable him to help the communities to organize themselves to meet such needs and catch a vision of this type of service. You can easily see how it would be a full time job for a person to fill these two needs. Peter Dyck reported on the effects which this type of service had on the persons from his community who served in North Topeka. He felt it has helped the members to see where they might serve those in need in their local communities. If this type of program can help our constituency regain their vision of true brotherhood and mutual aid, it will be worth all the efforts and funds which are invested.

I would certainly appreciate if you would also give this matter your consideration and take whatever action is necessary.

* * *

MCC continued its advisory role for several years.

Reading 44

<u>Executive Committee Meeting Minutes, March 12, 1955.</u>

In view of the growing interest and importance of the disaster service work, agreed to recommend to MCC Executive Committee that:

a. In view of the local nature of disaster work, MCC should encourage state, district, or provincial inter-Mennonite organizations to continue assuming the responsibility and initiative.

b. For the purposes of coordination of the work among these local groups and with the various constituent group programs, MCC should provide a coordination committee composed of a member of the Akron staff and representatives to be designated by their respective constituent groups.

c. Individual state, district, or provincial organizations, for interests and concerns affecting other organizations would channel such suggestions or questions to the coordination committee representative in Akron. This Coordination Committee may also call meetings of state, district or provincial representatives as necessary.

d. Since such inter-Mennonite disaster organizations are in effect affiliates of MCC, MCC should make an insignia available to Mennonite Disaster Service based on the MCC symbol.

e. In principle it would be desirable eventually to designate a single contact person for each Red Cross region to channel all Red Cross contacts with that office. Any contacts with the National Red Cross headquarters will be handled by the Akron staff.

f. MCC should take the initiative in any contacts with Civil Defense on the national level. Local or state organizations should clear with Akron before attempting contacts with the state or regional civil defense.

g. When disaster occurs in areas in which Mennonite Disaster Service is not organized, organizations nearest these regions should make investigation on their own or at the request of MCC, but in any case Akron is to be the clearing house.

h. Training for foremen and other specialized persons should be carried on on state, district, or provincial initiative with such help as available.

i. MCC recommend use of the name "Mennonite Disaster Service" to provincial, district, or state groups.

j. MCC facilitate information sharing by:

(i) being a center for information sharing

(ii) establishing a mailing list of all provincial and state committee members to be shared with officers of all state committees,

(iii) encouraging the sharing of reports on disasters and minutes either directly among state committee officers or with Akron facilitating by duplicating and mailing,

(iv) accumulating a supply of basic materials for sharing with new groups.

k. MCC assist disaster service in organizing by:

(i) sharing experience of other areas,

(ii) suggesting how the district, state, or provincial group might organize,

(iii) on recommendation of the coordinating committee, providing someone to assist groups in organizing and planning (this could be an interested person from a nearby area).

* * *

Later in 1955, after much debate, and in spite of the fears of loss of autonomy on the part of some local MDS groups, the regional groups appointed representatives to a national coordination committee under the auspices of MCC. During the same year Harry and Olga Martens traveled throughout the U.S., meeting congregations interested in MDS work, and explaining the organization. By 1962 MDS had become a section of MCC.

Harry Martens was national and international MDS coordinator on a volunteer basis from 1954-61. C. L. Graber served for six months after that and from 1962-65 Wayne Clemens was executive coordinator. Delmar Stahly and C. Nelson Hostetter served as executive coordinators after 1965. The following documents outline the organization and actual functioning of MDS.

Reading 45

DAY OF DISASTER, Katie Funk Wiebe. Scottdale: Herald Press, 1976, pp. 106-107.

The paid staff totals one person; all others volunteer their time. The organizational structure on any level, whether regional, national, or international, is maintained to serve a supportive and coordinating role rather than an administrative one. No orders come from the top, only guidelines for program planning and project operations.

The governing body of Mennonite Disaster Service is the MDS section of MCC which has eighteen members representing major Mennonite groups and includes the five regional directors. The section meets twice each year and elects an executive committee of five from among themselves to meet three to five times a year.

All local MDS units remain autonomous and arrive at their own decisions and formation of policy according to local needs. Each unit has a roster of officers, the chairman being responsible for the overall operations. The secretary-treasurer is assigned the listing of active congregational contact persons and raising basic finances and keeping records, not always considered important at first. "We just went out to work and then came home and plowed," said one coordinator.

The coordinator's duties are to relay information from the field director through the network to the congregations to set in motion the necessary logistics and to alert volunteers.

Reading 46

DAY OF DISASTER, Katie Funk Wiebe. Scottdale: Herald Press, 1976, Appendix C - Listing of MDS Units by Regions.

APPENDIX C

Listing of MDS Units by Regions

REGION I

1. Northern New York, 2. Western New York, 3. Penn-

York, 4. Eastern Pennsylvania, 5. Lancaster Area, Pennsylvania, 6. Cumberland Valley, Pennsylvania, 7. Western Pennsylvania and Maryland, 8. Delmarva Peninsula, 9. Tidewater, Virginia, 10. Shenandoah Valley, Virginia, 11. North Carolina and Eastern Tennessee, 12. South Carolina, 13. Alabama and Northwest Florida, 14. Central and South Florida, 15. Puerto Rico, 16. New England States, 17. Georgia.

REGION II

1. Wisconsin, 2. Michigan, 3. Illinois, 4. Indiana and Lower Michigan, 5. Western Ohio, 6. Eastern Ohio, 7. Kentucky and Tennessee, 8. Mississippi-Louisiana.

REGION III

1. Western Montana, 2. Eastern Montana, 3. North Dakota, 4. Northern Minnesota, 5. Minnesota, 6. South Dakota, 7. Nebraska, 8. Iowa, 9. Colorado, 10. Kansas, 11. Missouri, 12. Arkansas, 13. Oklahoma, 14. New Mexico, 15. South Texas.

REGION IV

1. Western Washington, 2. Eastern Washington, 3. Oregon, 4. Idaho, 5. California, 6. Arizona.

REGION V (CANADA)

Ontario, Manitoba, Saskatchewan, Alberta, British Columbia.

INTERNATIONAL

Honduras

* * *

In 1955 an MDS headquarters was established at Hesston, Kansas. Training schools for field directors were started in 1955, and a mobile office was added in 1956. The film "El Dorado," describing MDS activities, was produced in 1958. Rescue teams were trained and assembled in 1959, and radio equipment added in 1960.

MDS faced a series of theoretical as well as practical problems. Harry Martens outlined some of these in a speech given at the all-unit MDS Meeting in Phoenix, Arizona, February 10-11, 1978. In a section entitled "What were the big hurdles in the early days?", Martens listed the following:

1. To organize or not to organize.
2. To relate to the Red Cross or not to. (What about our witness?)
3. To relate to civil government (National Guard) or not to.
4. To relate to Civil Defense organizations (very potent question in the days of air raid shelters).
5. How to relate to MCC Akron (we want to be a grassroots organization).
6. How to organize to serve in disaster areas where we have few or no Mennonites (e.g., the deep South, abroad).

The following documents describe how some of these questions were resolved.

Reading 47

"Statement of Guiding Principles about Civil Defense." From HANDBOOK OF MANITOBA MENNONITE DISASTER SERVICE, 1960.

CIVIL DEFENSE

1. Civil Defense has been defined by the National Security Resources Board (U.S.A.) thus: "Civil Defense can be defined as the protection of the home front by civilians acting under civil authority to minimize casualties and war damage and preserve maximum civilian support of the war effort." Our interviews with Canadian officials indicate that the same definition would apply, in principle, to Civil Defense in Canada.

2. We find ourselves in full sympathy with the concern for human need which has contributed to the establishment of Civil Defense. But we must also recognize that "support of the war effort" is directly and inevitably involved in its establishment, motivation and operation, and that this is in conflict with our basic non-resistant commitment as Christians to follow peace with all men.

3. Under existing legislation, in certain emergencies which may be caused by war or natural disaster, Civil Defense may, by governmental decision, become a part of the chain of government action and even of military command. In such emergencies we must recognize the authority and the responsibility of Civil Defense personnel to administer and enforce the law, and must act as law-abiding citizens. However, if Divine law and the human law conflict, we must always obey God rather than men.

4. We recommend therefore to our people:

(1) That they refrain from membership in Civil Defense organizations, and from entering into such contracts or standing, binding agreements with them as may restrict freedom of action and testimony in accord with our Christian convictions; (2) That individuals such as amateur radio operators, fire fighters, medical and nursing personnel, or institutions such as hospitals and schools--if called upon--declare their willingness to render service in any emergency, and allow themselves to be registered for availability, but without becoming an integral part of Civil Defense or supporting its entire program; (3) That, in general, they cooperate with recognized governmental and private disaster organizations such as Civil Defense and the Red Cross which may be operating in a disaster area, where this can be done without violating the principles set forth in this statement; (4) That for the sake of clarity of position and testimony they train for service and render service through Mennonite channels wherever possible, both in peace and war.

/This statement was drafted and tentatively approved at

a joint meeting of the MCC Peace Section and Mennonite Disaster Service representatives at Chicago, Illinois, on March 1 and 2, 1956. It was completed and published by the MCC Peace Section./

Reading 48

DAY OF DISASTER, Katie Funk Wiebe. Scottdale: Herald Press, 1976, P. 102.

The definition of disaster was expanded to include the chronic as well as the acute crisis, destruction caused not only by nature, but also by acts of man. MDS . . . was the first disaster organization to send workers to repair houses in urban low-income areas, when it began working with Jeff-Vander-Lou, Inc., in St. Louis in 1967.

At present, community work, assisting disabled and disadvantaged persons, aiding in Headstart programs, and caring for disadvantaged children are all becoming worthy projects. Inner-city work, rehabilitating ghetto homes, continues to be an important aspect of MDS work.

URBAN WORK

MDS work in St. Louis with Jeff Vander Lou has come to a temporary halt pending resolution of union plans to build a block of houses in the area. The Indiana-Michigan MDS Unit is now the most active in cities, helping occasionally the East Central Area Improvement Association remodel homes in Fort Wayne. They are considering several projects in South Bend, having completed their commitment to Freedom Homes, Inc., at Grand Rapids. The spring agricultural activity has proven an increasing obstacle to recruitment of MDS workers for the Pittsburgh project to provide facilities for the United Black Front Organization. The Western Pennsylvania-Western Maryland Unit under Alton Miller is taking the lead in supplying men here, but we have requested help from Ontario and eastern Ohio.

Several tentative generalizations concerning MDS in the cities might be helpful at this point:

1. As Mennonites we do not identify easily with those of other races and poverty-stricken persons.

2. We have considerable ambivalence about our call to work in the cities, accepting the responsibility in theory but readily raising questions concerning specific programs and prospects for work.

3. Those who pioneer in actual urban situations and who experience a down-to-earth contact with individuals in extreme poverty, or of another race, usually feel that efforts to communicate through working together is very re-

warding; and they often seek additional opportunities for work experience.

* * *

MDS Youth Squads were organized for the summers of 1973, 1974, and 1975. These groups of young people spent ten weeks doing cleanup and rehabilitation at various places throughout the U.S. Traveling Youth Squads were also organized for periods of six months or longer.

As transportation became easier, MDS expanded its work to include foreign countries near the U.S. mainland.

The most important aspect of MDS has been its impact on those who volunteer to work, and on those whom they help.

Reading 49

DAY OF DISASTER, Katie Funk Wiebe. Scottdale: Herald Press, 1976, P. 46.

In locating projects, MDS keeps in mind a spiritual ministry as well as a material one. Deer Park, Louisiana, a community of 200 families, was chosen as a project site not only because it was inundated by Mississippi River floodwaters, but also because it had no Christian ministry, no church, not even any church buildings.

After immediate cleanup and repair tasks are completed, the long-term work begins for MDS volunteers, such as reconstruction of houses and other buildings. As MDS volunteers become more intimately involved with the community and as local people become acquainted with the MDS program, and see that one roof after another is being replaced, and as they come to know MDSers as Jerry, Ruth, and Bill, the bonds become stronger. The day MDS decides its work is finished is sometimes a painful one. The people want them to stay. But they have to go. They leave behind friends. And hope. And courage to begin again. And sometimes people who have decided to begin this new life in a clean house with faith in Jesus Christ.